FULLWOOD HALL

"A GOOD CAPITALE MANSION"

THE FIRST 600 YEARS

by

SUSAN HOSTOMBE

and

ALAN CRUTCH

CONTENTS

OWNERS AND OCCUPIERS OF FULLWOOD HALL

Year	Owners	Occupier	Notes	Monarchs and events
1283	William Lynott	William Lynott	First recorded owner of land in Fulwood	Henry III
1380	Adam and Isolda Lynott	Lynott family	Acquiring more land	Richard II
1391	John Lynott		Acquires land and settles a house and land on himself and his heirs. His heir is Adam Lynott	Richard II
1428	Agnes Lynott (Wife of John Fox)	Agnes, John, and their family	Agnes inherits Fullwood Hall (F H) on death of her father Adam Lynott	Henry VI
1456	Thomas Fox I	Fox family	Thomas Fox inherits F H on his mother Agnes's death	Wars of the Roses
1490	Thomas Fox II	Fox Family	Inherits on Thomas I's death	Henry VII
1508	Thomas Fox II	Fox Family	Okenhall land acquired	Henry VII
1515/6	Robert Fox		Inherits on Thomas II's death	Henry VIII
1537	Robert and Emmott Fox	Monks	The legend is that monks lived at F H for a year	Henry VIII Dissolution of the Monasteries
1543	Robert t Fox	Fox family	Transfers land to himself and his eldest son. William	Henry VIII
1544	William Fox I	Fox Family	Robert Fox dies. dispute arises between his widow Emmott and her son William Fox	Henry VIII
1580	William Fox II	Fox family	Inherits on William I's death	Elizabeth I
1587	William Fox II	Fox family	New landlord Thomas Howard Earl of Surrey	Elizabeth 1
1611	Ulysses Fox	Fox family	Inherits on William's death	James 1
1648	Ulysses Fox	Fox family	Death of Ulysses' heir, his son William Fox III	Charles 1 Civil War
1649	Trustees	Unknown	Death of Ulysses Fox Grandson George his heir	Charles 1 executed
1666	George Fox I	George Fox & family	George has reached 21, inherited and married Dorothy Balguy	Charles II Great fire of London
1691	William Fox IV	William and George Fox (Jr)	William inherits on his father George's death in 1691/2	William III 1688 Glorious Revolution
1698	George Fox II		George (Jr) buys out all his brother William's interest in FH	William III
1701	William Fox IV	Dies	William dies leaving a widow and 2 daughters.	William III
1701	George Fox II	Litigation	Brought by Anne Fox William's widow against George	William III
1707	John Fox	John Fox	F H is sold. John Fox is no relation to the previous owners	Anne
1721	Trustees of John Fox	Dorothy Oliver and husband	John Fox dies giving a life interest to his niece Dorothy. She later remarries George Hampton	George I South Sea Bubble

1746	Trustees of John Fox	George Hampton?	The Hall held on trust for 6 beneficiaries following Dorothy's death	George II
1752	Rev John Clarkson	George Hallam	Rev Clarkson buys F H as an investment	George II 11 days lost to the calendar
1757	Trustees of John Clarkson	George Hallam	FH held on trust for his 5 daughters after John's death	George II
1784 & '85	George Greaves	Robert Marshall (Dec 1784)	George Greaves buys copyhold of FH (1784) & Freehold (1785)	George III
1788	George B Greaves	Robert Marshall	15 years lease granted to Robert Marshall	George III Trafalgar 1805 Waterloo 1815
1834	John Greaves	John Marshall	John Greaves inherits FH freehold- his tenant is John Marshall	William IV
1859	Henry Marwood Greaves	John Marshall	Henry Marwood Greaves becomes landlord of FH	Victoria
1867	Henry Marwood Greaves	Robert Marshall	Becomes tenant on his father's death	Victoria
1878	"	Ann Marshall	Inherits tenancy on husband's death	Victoria
c1880	"	Thomas and Ann Brownhill	Ann has remarried	Victoria
1885	"	John Hutchinson	John buys FH tenancy at auction	Victoria
1891	"	Mary Hutchinson Frederick and Fanny Hawke	Mary is John's widow and Fanny her married daughter	Victoria
1897	Frederick and Goody Oates	Oates Family	Hall tenancy bought with money from Fred's mother's estate	Victoria's Diamond Jubilee
1915	Frederick Oates	Arthur Cooper	Goody Oates dies. Frederick retires to Blackpool. Sublets FH	George V WWI 1914-8
1926	Exors Fred Oates	Arthur Cooper	Frederick dies in Blackpool buried in Fulwood Churchyard	George V
1930	Exors Fred Oates	Ben Cooper and family	Ben Cooper takes over the farm from his father	George V
1931	Benjamin Cooper	Ben Cooper and family	Ben Cooper buys the Hall from the Greaves family. He already has the tenancy	Depression Abdication Edward VIII
1944	Morgan and Doris Fairest	Morgan Fairest and family	Morgan Fairest buys the Hall	George VI WWII 1939-45
1964	Doris Fairest	Doris Fairest and Susan Fairest	Morgan & his elder son Derry die, Susan is Derry's daughter	Elizabeth II 1953-2022
1968	Doris Fairest Trustees	None	FH empty for the next 4 years after Doris's death. Her chauffeur acts as caretaker of F H	Elizabeth II
1972	Barry & Dorothy Fairest	Barry Fairest and family	Barry is Morgan's surviving son and moves into F H with his family	Elizabeth II
1983	Roger & Sue Hostombe	Hostombe family	Buys FH at auction & in 1984 acquires The Firs & 3 Oakney fields	Elizabeth II Charles III 2022-

View of the Mayfield Valley from the Hall.

INTRODUCTION

by SUSAN HOSTOMBE

Our story about Fullwood Hall begins with the Court Rolls of the Manor of Sheffield in 1283 (Henry the third), when William, son of Simon Lynott, gave two shillings to hold three acres of land in Fullwood which appears to be where our house now stands. Over the next 145 years the Rolls record transactions by Robert, Isola (wife of Adam), John and Thomas Lynott.

The Lynott family farmed this land for several generations and, prior to the 1400's, they used local stone to build their home, some of the fabric of which remains today as part of the present house.

Since authorities agree that the surname Lynott was of old French origin the inference might be drawn that the original Lynott came over either with, or soon after, William the Conqueror.

The male line came to an end with the death of Adam Lynott in 1428 and the property passed to his daughter Agnes. She is mentioned in the Court Rolls of the Manor of Sheffield in the sixth year of the reign of Henry VI.

Agnes had married John Fox in 1392 and, from the time of her inheritance, their descendants lived at Fullwood Hall for almost 300 years

The story of Fullwood Hall ownership unfolds over the coming pages and brings us, 600 years later, to the current owner – my husband Roger Hostombe - another name of French origin.

We came to live in this lovely old place in 1983 and the history held within these walls continues to fascinate me. I am intrigued to think about daily life here over the many years and I love the stories, the facts and the legends associated with the house.

I imagine the occupants receiving news of what would become historic events and gathering to discuss them by candlelight in these same rooms, probably sitting by the fire as I do now. I think about the Fox family living here in 1461 during the Wars of the Roses and I wonder about their hopes and fears. Two hundred years later, in 1620, would the family have known about the Pilgrim Fathers setting off for America when Ulysses Fox was busy with his renovations?

I love the stone walls – two to three feet thick, the small mullioned windows, oak panelling, low lintels, and beams. Not a single wall is straight, and all the rooms are small and cosy.

It is a welcoming and comforting place where Roger and I are so fortunate in being the current custodians.

The house is not far from the village of Fulwood and I am often asked about the double 'L' in Fullwood Hall. My favourite explanation goes back to the time of Richard I - 'the Lionheart' (1189 – 1199). At this time this area of Fulwood and

Rivelin, lying so close to Loxley, was allegedly where Robin Hood made his first essays in 'chasing the fallow deer.' Robin was perhaps a legend, but this area was mainly woodland all those years ago and the area was called Fullwood. The house being so much older than the village has retained the ancient spelling. . . and who knows – perhaps Robin did shoot his first deer in the full wood!

Moving to the more recent past I found myself intrigued by such stories and history. I began to make notes and collect all the information I could discover about the house and its occupants. As my collection grew I decided to make it into some form of booklet which could be passed down the generations of our family and to the many people who have expressed interest in the house. It was, and now is, my hope that this little volume will be kept and added to by those privileged to live here in the future and whom I trust will love, cherish, and enjoy the house as we do.

The Covid pandemic lockdowns of 2020 left me with no more excuses regarding my project and a time-consuming and enjoyable period ensued as I made copious notes and placed all my information into files. Barry Fairest had kindly written several letters to me over the years describing his memories of living here, though unfortunately all the Fairest paperwork relating to Fullwood Hall was destroyed in a warehouse fire in 1984. The names of Marshall, Oates and Cooper were familiar to me and of course the Fox family, but I still had gaps in the occupancy especially around the eighteen hundreds.

I needed assistance – but who to ask?

By great chance and good fortune Roger came across a book with a photo of Fullwood Hall on the cover which I felt was an excellent account of local history, houses and events written by Alan Crutch. I discovered that Alan lived nearby, and as I walked around the Oakney fields during "lockdown" I kept wondering whether he might possibly be willing to help me complete my project.

When the Covid restrictions lifted during the summer of 2021 Alan came to visit us here at Fullwood Hall one lovely summer's morning. The result, to my absolute delight, was that not only did Alan agree to help me but he has extended and brought very much more depth to my research – and, most importantly, he has managed to fill in all the gaps of ownership!

My passion for the architecture and history of the house itself has led to a recent succession of fascinating visits to Fullwood Hall by a variety of specialists, archivists, archaeologists, dendro-chronologists, and other enthusiasts.

The following pages are an amalgamation of these recent studies, my notes and files, and Alan's tireless research and enthusiasm for which I am most grateful.

INTRODUCTION

by ALAN CRUTCH

Ever since my family and I moved to Fulwood in 1983 I have been intrigued by Fullwood Hall, so it was with a mixture of surprise and pleasure that I received the invitation to contribute to this book.

It has always seemed to me that the Hall hides itself from the road. It lies in the lee of a hill, turning its back to Harrison Lane, to face the wonderful views over the Mayfield Valley. Its fields spread out both before and behind the Hall. Such an iconic building hides its secrets well. Why was it built there, like that, and what is its history?

Fullwood Hall from Harrison Lane

As you walk on the raised path next to Harrison Lane or drive along the road itself, you have a steep wooded bank on one side and the stone back wall of the Hall boundary on the other. Set into this wall is a small green door where the words 'Fullwood Hall' appear. As Sue has already pointed out, it is spelt with a double L because that was the original name of the Hall. Fulwood village developed significantly later and never adopted the second L. In this book therefore 'Fullwood' is used to describe the Hall and 'Fulwood' is the settlement shown on maps of the area. However, to return to the narrative, near to the door, on the Hall side of the wall, is a tall flagpole from which a flag sometimes flies. It is usually the Union flag but, for a period in summer 2022, it was the Ukrainian flag that flew above the Hall.

Apart from that all you will see is the massive stone slates of the roof, some tall elegant chimneys and a brief glimpse of some very old-looking windows and stonework.

When you think you have walked, or driven, past the Hall in either direction, you will find an entrance. The front entrance has substantial old gateposts and a gate. You peek down the drive to try to get a glimpse of the Hall but are frustrated as the drive leads to the garage. You see a small part of the garden but very little else in respect of the Hall itself. You will have no more success looking down the other entrance. The drive at the rear leads down a spectacular avenue of trees but comes out by the stable yard at the Hall.

Back driveway to the Hall. A painting by Caroline Holley

No matter how you try to catch a glimpse of it, the Hall remains elusive. It looks out over its own fields, all the way down to the small Congregational Chapel and the former Mayfield Environmental Centre, which was once the school for many children of the Mayfield Valley. A complete view can only be had, from a considerable distance; as you stand on Mayfield Road and look up to where the Hall stands high above you, in front of the trees on the hill above.

This brief introduction will try to answer the questions posed earlier. Why was the Hall built where it was? Why does it lie so far below the road? Very little has been written about Fullwood Hall. Although the date 1428 is mentioned and 1620 is often stressed, precious little detail exists of the Hall itself or its occupants.

The Hall guards its secrets closely. This book will, at least, make you realise that the 1620 date is a significant one in the history of the Hall, but it is far from the beginning of the story. Read on to find out more. .

The Hall is built very near to the point where the sandstone is exposed and the fields below are on clays and mudstone.[1] This is ideal because the stone for building can be extracted from on the doorstep and the fields below are good for agriculture. Fresh water springs flow freely in the area and one such spring ran next to where the Hall was built. Another ran through the fields to provide water for crops and animals. As a result, there were few better places to build. The lee near the top of the hill provided shelter, high quality, fresh water, and plentiful stone. Add to that the view across the Mayfield Valley and you have an almost perfect combination for a place to make your home. Almost perfect? Well, this is Yorkshire and sometimes winters here are not for the faint-hearted.

The other question asked in this section of the book, concerns the siting of the Hall below the road. It is a trick question as the Hall existed long before Harrison Lane was constructed. In the mid-eighteenth century the Hall was open onto a Common. As part of the Sheffield Enclosure Act many proper roads were made, including what is now Harrison Lane in the 1790's. The road was formed by building up the ground level behind the Hall. This raised the road very much above the ground floor of the Hall. A boundary wall was built to ensure privacy. That is the arrangement that you see today. The name of the road came from the Harrison family who lived at Bole Hill Farm.

Until the road was constructed the oldest part of the Hall would have been clearly visible to anyone coming up the hill to the Common which spread across three sides of the Hall and was then known as Fullwood Hall Common. This common, together with those at Birks Green, near Bennet Grange, School Green, next to Fulwood Old School, and Brook House Green in Fulwood all disappeared as a result of the desire to improve communications to Fulwood. The name of the new road that was suggested by the three Commissioners appointed to implement the Enclosure Act was Fulwood Road, a name it still bears for part of its length. The new road passed Fullwood Hall on the way to its destination at Birk's Green and that part of the road is now called Harrison Lane. [2]

Near the side gate there are two intriguing blocked-up windows incorporated into the wall. This section of the wall was once a part of a sizeable building that stood there, right next to the common, before the level of the road was so substantially raised in the 1790's. The windows would have belonged to an upper floor given how far below the present wall the oldest part of Fullwood Hall stands. The old building was certainly there in 1791 as it is shown on plans of that date.

This book will contain stories of a rags to riches rise, a dissipated fall, tragedies, arguments within the family and with neighbours, a fatal accident near the Hall, a dog kennel built of stone, messages from a nearby hill, and the odd ghost or two. Even the Dragon of Wantley and Robin Hood make appearances! There are also several excellent paintings and other representations of various features and of the Hall itself.

First though, it is time to read about some of the stories and legends that have been passed down from owner to owner before we are introduced to a little early history of the land on which the Hall stands and the earliest references to a house and a Hall in Fulwood. The photograph below sets the scene for the next chapter which describes the rumours stories and legends associated with the Hall.

---

1   The geology of the land on which the Hall stands is contained in Appendix 1
2   Colin Cooper Old Fulwood (3) in Articles on Old Fulwood cuttings and his notes donated by him to Sheffield Local studies Library

Not for the faint-hearted?

CHAPTER 1

RUMOURS STORIES & LEGENDS

It is hardly surprising that Fullwood Hall has its fair share of stories handed down from one generation to the next. Some families have lived there for centuries, many children have been born there and it has provided a source of employment for local people since at least the Middle Ages. That is the period that is the source of the first legend.

Robin of Loxley (aka Robin Hood) was reported to have hidden in the Rivelin valley and other local woods to escape the law following the murder of his father-in-law. This was whilst he was being sheltered by his mother who lived in nearby Loxley. It is claimed that Robin was born at Little Haggas Croft in that village in the year 1190 (although other versions are available). As already mentioned, one of the twentieth century owners of the Hall, Dorothy Fairest, proudly claimed to the present owners that Robin Hood killed his first deer in the Full Wood, the forest that was still extensive in the area in those days, and from which Fullwood Hall acquired its name. One of Robin's closest companions, Little John, is reputed to be buried at nearby Hathersage Church – one of the places where the early Hall occupants went to celebrate their births and marriages and to attend family funerals probably following the track past where Stanage Pole now stands.

Whatever the truth of the stories about Robin, do not be too hasty in dismissing a local connection in favour of Nottingham. That location was invented by Walter Scott in the nineteenth century.

As will later be seen, religion has played a prominent role in the history of the house. Fulwood did not have an 'establishment' church until well into the nineteenth century so tended to go its own way in religious matters. Yorkshire was not quick to accept the abandonment of the old Catholic religion and its traditions and there is no reason to think that the occupants of Fullwood Hall were any different. There is certainly a tradition that monks and lay brothers working in the nearby fields, used to take meals at an ancient stone table (part of which is now the cellar of Fullwood Hall). There is a further handed-down story that Fullwood Hall was occupied for a year by monks in the time of Thomas Cromwell. This would presumably be those made homeless by the Dissolution. This was a common phenomenon throughout the country at this time so may well be true. The tale suggests that those who had control of the Hall held on to the old religion, even when it became a punishable offence to aid priests administering the rights of the Catholic Church.

Given the dangers at various times in history, Catholic support would have been risky but Fullwood was a very out of the way place in those days and there were probably plenty of people who still clung to the old ways. It is therefore possible that these stories are true. A further legend handed down was that anyone damaging the stone table would suffer bad luck, and this does seem to have come true as the family responsible for breaking up the table in the twentieth century did indeed receive more than their fair share of misfortune. The table is described as 'an heirloom' in a will dated 1648 which also stated that it must remain in the Hall. Fortunately for the family responsible for the damage, most of the table remains intact and a substantial part of it now stands in the cellar at the Hall. Other parts seem to have been incorporated into internal features of the Hall, so, at least, remain in the building.

Rounded end of stone table now in the Hall cellar

Further evidence of a priestly connection may be supplied by an upstairs bedroom in the Hall which still has an alcove set into the area above the stairs, which may have been a prayer niche. The same room also had a vertical stone coffin cupboard incorporated into one of the thick external stone walls where a coffin would be stored in readiness for need when the time came. The stone cupboard was only removed in the twentieth century, many years after any coffin that may have been stored there.

There are two further tales with priestly connections. The first links Fullwood Hall with Priest Hill, which is a prominent hill visible from the Hall. It is said that when the authorities were searching for priests in the area, they would usually approach from that direction and those that lived on Priest Hill would send a signal to the occupants of Fullwood Hall that danger was imminent. This leads directly to the second tale which concerns a passage or tunnel leading from Fullwood Hall to Bennett Grange. Both houses certainly date back to the Elizabethan period or beyond and there are people who were alive in the early years of the twentieth century who remember playing in parts of a tunnel from each of the two houses.

One of the aims of this book is to investigate the stories associated with Fullwood Hall as well as its physical features. Those investigations will form a separate chapter towards the end of the book, but first it is interesting to point out that R. Perret reported a possible rising midwinter-sun alignment which is visible from Bole Hill to Priest Hill, then to Castle Dyke and finishing at Beauchief Abbey. [3] The line passes directly over Fullwood Hall. It is not uncommon in pre-history for fires to have been lit on summits such as the above that were each visible to its neighbouring hilltop. This was done to celebrate the beginnings of the sun's return towards its midsummer position on the horizon. Maybe that happened here and the tales of signs and passages are folk memories going back into pre-history to commemorate this link between places.

It is impossible to leave this section without some mention of the supernatural. It will come as no surprise that given the age of the Hall, there are reports of the appearance of ghosts and strange phenomena. Two horses from the Hall stables appeared terrified by the water troughs on Harrison Lane and absolutely refused to go anywhere near them. There is a local tale of a man being hanged there and a local girl believed herself to be dragged off her horse by an unseen presence by the troughs. That area certainly seems to attract more than its fair share of rumour and superstition. Maybe it was this aura that the horses were picking up!

It is reported by Valerie Salim that a ghostly carriage has been seen rattling on its way along Harrison Lane outside Fullwood Hall pursued by a female ghost. [4] One of the recent occupants of the Hall reports a ghostly lady, wearing a long dress, standing at the foot of the bed. She is described as seeming kindly rather than frightening. Things move to unexpected places or just disappear and reappear after a day or two. It would therefore seem that any influences are not malevolent. Maybe they could be called just high-spirited!

---

3   *This is reported by David Clarke in his book 'Strange South Yorkshire' p 107*
4   *Ghost Hunters Guide to Sheffield Valerie Salim p83*

Fullwood Hall in Winter

CHAPTER 2

EARLY YEARS
and
The Lynott and the Fox families

1283 to 1537

An Archaeological survey carried out on behalf of the Friends of the Porter Valley in 2001 [5] discovered the bottom courses of a field wall at Fullwood Hall to be made up partly of very large boulders and upright stones that indicate occupation of that part of the site possibly as early as the Romano-British period (c100-410 AD). There is an even larger boulder at the base of another wall, in the Oakney fields, not covered by the survey.

Oakney field boulder

The same survey reports that it is likely that from masonry, pottery and other objects found there was a Romano-British farm in the vicinity of School Green Lane,[6] just a few yards down the road from Fullwood Hall. It is therefore certainly

---

5   *Porter Valley Landscape History and Archaeology Final Report April 2004. Feature 10 p30*
6   *Ibid s5. 2 p9*

possible that the Fullwood Hall site may have been occupied during that period, even though the earliest known reference to this land being cultivated in the region is from 1283. [7]

In the centuries either side of the Norman Conquest, in 1066, the whole area, known as Rivelin Chase, was a popular hunting region for local Lords, both Norman and Saxon. [8] By the time of the Tudors, Wardens of the Game were appointed[9]. No doubt one of their duties, and those of their predecessors, was to keep an eye out for poachers and outlaws like Robin Hood and Little John.

Historic Fulwood in Hallam does not appear to have been solely about the pleasures of the hunt, and helping oneself to deer. It is reported as a place where oxen were kept for the Lord of the Manor in the twelfth century[10] and the White Canons of nearby Beauchief Abbey are recorded as having a grange in Fulwood[11]. It is therefore certain that farming was being carried on in the region both for the benefit of the Lord of the Manor and for, and by, the religious community from the Abbey. As a result of various gifts, the Abbey was given free pasturage in the region including for 'all manner of cattle, except goats'. They were also allowed to erect 'cow-houses' and take grasses for the purpose of thatching their buildings[12].

The White Canons' or Premonstratensian White Canons, to give them their Sunday name, first settled in Beauchief in 1176. They were not monks in the strictest sense of the word but they were active in their local communities and were identifiable by their white habits and caps. Beauchief housed an Abbott and up to 23 canons, 8 Chantry priests and an unknown number of lay brothers[13] who worked at the granges and on other land and operations that the Abbey controlled. As well as Fulwood Grange, it is possible that they owned, and worked on, some of the land currently belonging to Fullwood Hall and it may well be that what is now Fullwood Hall land formed part of the de Furnival gifts to the Canons at Beauchief Abbey of 'all their land in Fulwood.'

The Abbey also probably controlled nearby iron smelting, mineral extraction, woodland industries, and mills. The smelting at Bole Hill near Bole Hill Farm, within yards of Fullwood Hall, may well have been operating under their control.

No plans are available, but the relatively few local Court Rolls that have survived from 1277 onwards, provide evidence of local land transactions and individuals who had a right to occupy land of the Lord of the Manor as well as on what terms. This gives us an indication of some of the history of at least part of what is now Fullwood Hall land.

As well as the 3 acres of land at Fulwood acquired by William Lynott in 1283, the Lynotts (or Linots) seem to have settled in Fullwood. In 1297 Robert Linot is

---

7   *Colin Cooper 'David Lane' in Articles on Old Fulwood cuttings and his notes donated by him to Sheffield Local studies Library*

8   *Rev Joseph Hunter the History and Topography of the Parish of Sheffield Hallamshire 1819 p220-222*

9   *Ibid p220-222*

10   *At Fullwood Booth according to Dr Pegge's "History of Beauchief Abbey"*

11   *Ibid Given by Gerald de Furnival and later by his son, with other land in Fulwood. The grange is thought to have been on the site of the present Fulwood Grange.*

12   *Pegge History of Beauchief Abbey p134-201*

13   *J Edward Vickers The Old & Historical Buildings of Sheffield p32*

reported as paying a tax levy of £3 5s 6d as a tax subsidy[14] payable at the rate of one ninth of all the goods 'in his field, house and elsewhere', that he owned on the feast day of St Michael's last past. Over the years, the Lynott family acquired substantial possessions including the Beauchief Abbey Grange in Fulwood as well as property in Sheffield. One branch almost certainly lived in a house in the Fulwood area but it is impossible to tell where they lived. It is though more than likely to have been part of what is now Fullwood Hall.

The family seem to have avoided the worst predations of the Black Death of 1349 when up to half of England's population are estimated to have died, and that of 1360-61 when the estimation is up to a further 20%. It is reported that those plagues reduced the number of lay brothers at the Abbey to such an extent that the Abbey moved from having lay brothers working their farms to renting the farms to local farmers. [15] This may well have benefitted those living in Fulwood.

Beauchief Grange in Fullwood was being farmed by Robert and Adam Linnot according to the poll tax returns for 1379 for which they paid 3 times more than their neighbours. [16] In the following year, Isola, the wife of the above Adam Lynott took ½ bevet[17] of Hastler land and two acres and one rood of Mattock Land in Fulwood for the term of her life, for a fee of 4 shillings. [18] This certainly proves that the Lynott family were farming in Fulwood at this time. The above land was copyhold from the Lord of the Manor and seems to be an addition to an already substantial farming enterprise.

'Hastler land' is an interesting phrase which refers to ancient farmland, the holder of which had important local rights such as being able to elect the local constable[19]. The ownership also seems to have brought with it an obligation of military service to the Lord of the Manor. There is evidence of this happening at Fullwood Hall as late as 1637. The reference to this sort of land shows that farming was being carried on in Fulwood well before 1380. Mattock land refers to the tool that was needed to break up moorland so that it could be farmed.[20]

In the fifteenth year of the reign of Richard II (1391) there is the first mention of the Lynotts having a house in Fulwood. In that year John Lynott surrenders

'One Messuage with ½ acre of land and a meadow... [the wonderfully named Woodcock Pighill] with a parcel of land in Okinholt'

Surrender was then how property was transferred, so by this transaction he was assigning the house and land to himself and his heirs. It is intriguing to think that may well be the first reference we have to what is now Fullwood Hall.

John Lynott's heirs certainly inherited the property. Adam Lynott was probably John's son, and on his death the family house at Fullwood passed to his own

---

14   The ninth of Edward 1
15   Pegge History of Beauchief Abbey p131
16   David Hey Historic Hallamshire pp 73-4 for a summary of the Lynott family
17   bevet or bovate refers to the amount of land that could be ploughed by one ox in a season. This varied from place to place but would probably have been between 8 and 15 acres
18   The amounts referred to in this section are the customary fees paid on registration in the Rolls rather than the amount paid for the land itself.
19   David Hey Historic Hallamshire p20-23 which gives an excellent summary of tenant farmers in the area at this time.
20   ibid p21.

daughter Agnes. The Court roll entry for 6th Henry VI (1428) records Agnes as being the last of the Lynotts to hold land in Fulwood.

'To hold of the Lord (of the Manor) 1 messuage and ½ covet of Hastler land in Fulwood and 1 parcel of Hastler land in Hallam after the death of Adam Lynott whose heir she is[21]*'*

Agnes' husband at the time (1428) was John Fox but it is clear she owned the land in her own right as she was paying for 'Pannage in Ryvelynn' in 1441. 'Pannage' is a term for the feeding of swine. At that time the Rivelin valley included the Mayfield Valley, so she had the right to let her pigs forage in the Lord's local woodland.

Her husband John Fox had acquired one parcel of Hastler land called Okenhall in his own right in 1439. This was part of the Oakney fields above Fullwood Hall. It is more than likely that John and Agnes were living in the family home, the house of her parents Adam and Isolda Lynott.

The Wars of the Roses that were fought intermittently between 1428 and 1485 have led to an absence of many records of this period. It is impossible to know whether the family were called upon to fight for either side in the dynastic struggles of that time but those conflicts may have been a cause of the failure of the male line of the Lynotts. References to that name disappear almost completely from the Court Rolls after Adam's death in 1428, apart from in 1441 when a Thomas de Karre *'drew blood from John Lynot, against the peace for which Thomas was fined 6s 8d'*. John Lynot himself was being distrained[22] and was fined one shilling at the same court for playing at *'dice and panning'* with William de Holdene, who was only fined 4d. The Fox name, (usually written ffox) only appears in the (very incomplete) Court Rolls after John Fox's marriage to Agnes Lynott but it became the surname that was to be associated with Fullwood Hall for the best part of the next 300 years.

Agnes and John Fox had a son, Thomas, who inherited the family interest in the property in 1456. His son, also called Thomas, inherited from his father in 1490 and acquired further Okenhall land for the estate in 1508.

By that time the Tudor dynasty was well established under Henry VII, and there was certainly a substantial house on site, by then being described as 'a Hall' in the Court Rolls.

The next occupant of the Hall was Robert Fox. He inherited from his father Thomas in 1515/6. He lived in what can only be described as 'interesting' times, but first we will consider how Fullwood Hall may have appeared in those early days.

---

21   *Liber Finium Customarionum (as translated by the Hunter Archaeological Society Proceedings (1918) vol I p286*

22   *Distrained here means summonsed to attend under a threat of a penalty*

CHAPTER 3

THE EARLY HALL

After a description of the legends concerning Fullwood Hall and our introduction to the Lynotts and the Foxes, this chapter will attempt to explain why we have subtitled this book 'The first 600 years' and to show how the Hall will have appeared all those centuries ago.

There is plenty of evidence to support occupation by the Fox family on the site of what is now Fullwood Hall for the whole period of that family's occupation beginning in the 1420's and for their predecessors, the Lynotts, from the 1390's. There are clues both inside the Hall and externally, but trying to piece together the evidence to obtain a clear picture of how the Hall may have appeared, and then changed, over the last six centuries was proving quite a challenge to the authors.

Documentary evidence consisted of the few surviving Court Roll entries already mentioned and the fact that the old title deeds for Fullwood Hall, held in the Rylands Library in Manchester, included 16 copies of Court Roll entries recorded in the records of the Manor of Sheffield not all of which have survived anywhere else. Each of these copies were originally handed to the new owner following their paying the appropriate fee to the Lord of the Manor. This was the fore-runner of the system of conveyancing that we are familiar with. The fact that these copies were bundled up together with the first conveyances and other documents relating to the Hall provides early evidence of entitlement of the Foxes to their home at Fullwood Hall and its estate. The earliest of these documents is dated 1439 and the latest is 1666. From this source it has been possible to piece together the continuous ownership of Fullwood Hall by the Fox family There is also the confirmation in the Court records themselves of Agnes Fox inheriting the house in Fulwood that previously belonged to her father back in 1391 and which she inherited in 1428

The current appearance of the Hall itself shows different building styles. It has internal oak beams that look very old and contain strange markings. Some internal stone fireplaces and archways are also of considerable age. There is also the story of the old stone table in the cellar which once may have been a refectory table around which monks gathered at mealtimes. All the above will be mentioned again in later chapters. Together these pieces of evidence had led us to the conclusion that most of the present Hall is much older than the 1620 plaque that stands above the front door has suggested to some previous writers about the Hall.

We needed help to enable us to fit what we had into a coherent story of the beginning, and subsequent growth, of the Hall. Assistance came from a dendro-chronological report prepared by Alison Arnold and Robert Howard of the Nottingham Tree-dating laboratory and David Cook's report from the Yorkshire Vernacular Building Studies Group.

The dendro-chronological report tested the timbers of some of the Hall's oak roof-truss timbers. Unfortunately, many of the beams, including the substantial downstairs oak beams were thought unsuitable for testing as they did not have the final growth rings of the tree from which they were cut. Without these rings the date the tree was felled cannot be ascertained. We knew that Fullwood Hall had work done on the roof in the early 1700's and again in the 1780's so were worried that nothing of significant age might be found.

However, when the report arrived, early dates were found for several roof timbers. Two samples came from trees felled in the period 1500-1520, another was from a tree felled in 1569, and one came from a tree felled in 1589. There were also several that returned dates shortly before 1620. These findings indicated roofing work in the early Tudor period, further work in the early and late Elizabethan times and other alterations in the Jacobean era'

Roof truss in attic and dendro-chronological samples

The photo shows what is called a closed truss with a central Kingpost. It was to be one of the most important pieces of evidence in enabling the Yorkshire Vernacular Buildings Study Group (YVBSG) to identify what sort of building Fullwood Hall was in the early 1500's. Before that the house would have been a typical medieval Hall.

It seems that Fullwood Hall was, by the early Tudor age, a half-timbered house, similar in many respects, to Bishops' House in Meersbrook Park Sheffield. Fullwood had an open Hall with an upstairs retreat known as a Solar. This would have been at the southerly end of the building, whilst anyone in the hall downstairs, at the north end, would have had an uninterrupted view up to the roof timbers. The roof truss shown in the illustration would have been visible and a decorative feature of the building along with other similar trusses, one of which still remains in the Hall attic. Some of the truss timbers have been replaced over the years, but the basic shape and arrangement have been retained.

The Hall's stone external walls may well have reached up to the roof of the medieval building that is likely to have stood on the present Hall site. Those stone walls are now limited to the first six courses but may well have formed the base for the later half-timbered house with the gaps in the oak external timbers filled in with stone or plaster up to the roof level. This sort of house was very fashionable in the Tudor period. At that time Fullwood Hall would have been high enough for a floor to be added to allow the construction of an upstairs Solar where the family could enjoy some privacy. The roof itself will have been covered by the large stone slates that were readily available locally and which are still used today. There was probably a device called a fire or smoke hood for diverting smoke from out of the Hall in the north-western corner, and access would have been from a door and lobby, or porch, at the north-east end of the building. The few windows would have been unglazed with what were known as window-cloths and wooden shutters to help keep out the worst of the Yorkshire weather.

The six levels of large blocks of dressed stone to the south and east still remain and may well have been part of the even earlier house occupied by the Lynott family as far back as 1391.

All the above features are shown in an excellent illustration by Allan Adams and, is itself based on the features found by YVBSG[23]. The drawing is reproduced here with his and their kind permission.

---

23   Yorkshire Vernacular Building Preservation Group

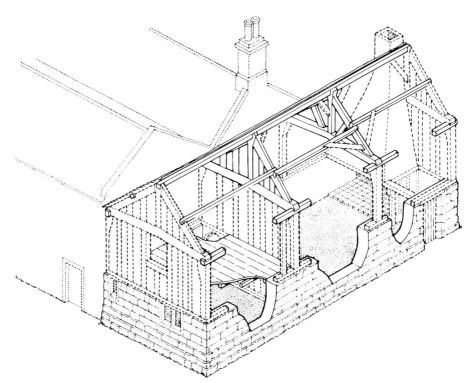

The Tudor Fullwood Hall pen and ink drawing by Allan Adams

Helpful notes concerning the drawing have also been provided by David Cook of YVBSG.

<u>Summary and drawing conventions used.</u> This drawing is designed to show the E wing in 1500-1525, when the roof was probably replaced by what is shown here. Assuming this is a replacement roof, then there must have been a building here before that, and there is some evidence for this in the historic documents. It's possible that the lower stone courses remain from this building. The layout from 1500-25 is one of an open hall forming the central and NE bay, and a solar (an upper floored room) to the SW bay.

The solid bold lines indicate timber work which exists to this day and some of the timbers have been scientifically dated. The dashed lines are other parts of these dated structures known to have existed from the evidence of empty mortice slots or are likely to have existed given our understanding of such buildings. The dotted lines are of the existing stonework to give context.

<u>Truss II.</u> Our starting point, because it has the best evidence, is the king post roof truss with angled struts - the second from the right in the drawing. The truss is numbered 'II' with precise and clear carpenters' marks. This is labelled truss 3 (purely for identification) by NTRDL. It is dated 1500-1525 by dendrochronology.

The drawing shows the arrangement before the principal rafter on the right was replaced in 1569/70. Then, the two purlins shown between NTRDL truss 3 and 2 were replaced by a single purlin. Both the 1569/70 principal rafter and presumably its contemporary purlin remain today. The tie beam has no empty mortices in the soffit for studs, so there was no timber partition wall below it.

'Truss I'. Going back to the current NE stone gable, we can tell that this would have been another roof truss in its place from the evidence of the angled empty mortice in the roof ridge beam. This would have been for a brace up from what would have been a king post there in 1500-1525. We can assume that this was truss I and would have been a closed truss forming the gable end of the wing, with a probable timber stud wall below. This is dashed in.

Truss III. Further down the roof there is an existing truss with vertical timber studs. This has grooves in the sides of the timbers for boards and was therefore a closed truss. The boards would have been flush with the SW or solar side. It's probable that there was a timber stud wall below this, but we can't see any evidence for it because the soffit (underside) of its tie beam is buried in the loft floor. This is labelled truss 2 (purely for identification) by NTRD but has a scratched carpenter's mark, 'III.' It could not be dated by dendrochronology but fits in with the 1500-1525 roof structure, so is very likely to be of this date.

There are no empty mortices from the post up to the ridge on the solar side.

'Truss IIII'. Next to the SW stone gable wall is a different truss type. This is a relatively simple principal rafter and tie beam truss. It is labelled truss 1 by NTRDL and a tree (or trees) was felled in 1618 to make the timbers. This is clearly a later replacement for what is shown in the drawing which is a gable-end closed truss of the same type as truss I, and which would have been truss IIII. The window dashed-in in the SW gable is conjectural – we have no evidence for it.

Fire hood at the NE end. This is dashed in. ... the building must have had some heating, and a fire hood is the most likely for this region. The dotted tile floor is conjectural.

External door. This is dashed in – it would have been in the regular position for this type of building and layout, forming a small entrance lobby against the side wall of the fire hood. A ... painting shows this end of the building with a long catslide roof over a front outshut...

Kitchen ceiling cross beam. Not shown in the drawing. This has joists in to it on both sides, numbered on the SW side. It also has a series of empty mortices (for a stud wall) and very deep chamfers. [The writers have noticed that at Bishops House in Meersbrook Park there is an identical arrangement where the mortices terminate above a doorway].

Solar floor/ceiling over the Morning Room. Shown with solid lines but presumed based on the evidence of the roof trusses above, and our understanding of these buildings – i.e., it is highly likely that there would have been an upper floor over at least one bay of the building. The arched door shown dashed in from the open hall to the room below the solar is conjectural.

Wall posts. We don't have any evidence for wall posts – so these are all dashed in. It seems likely that the upper floor was a timber construction due to the change in stone work above the very large lower courses.

Lower stone wall courses and gable windows. The walls are of very large stones, on a substantial stepped plinth. They may be part of a 15th C building given the rules of stratigraphy (what's underneath is oldest) and the date of the roof structure, above.

In summary therefore, there is likely to have been a medieval building that was converted in the period 1500-1525 into a half-timbered Tudor house which was entered through a doorway at the north-east end of the Hall. A fire would have burnt in a grate (possibly with an iron fireback) upon the tiled hearth near the northern gable wall. In the drawing there is a small lobby shown inside the entrance. On further inspection of the stonework by the writers, it seems to be more likely that there was an external porch rather than an internal lobby.

Once inside and looking upwards you would see the roof trusses and beams and a large fire hood some distance above the grate to take the wood-smoke away from the interior of the Hall. It looks as though it was screened off by a timber and board partition most likely with doors or open spaces to allow access and for the heat to pass through into the hall.

At the southern end of the building there was an area at first floor level where the owner and his family could have their privacy. This was called the Solar which was hidden from view by means of upright timbers with grooves into which boards were fitted with plaster between the boards. There may have been a window allowing the family to see what was going on downstairs in the Hall. The bed would probably have been a four-poster. Other, lesser, beds would be in the Hall. Privacy was not an option for most living in this era.

It is possible that Bishops' House in Meersbrook was constructed along similar lines to Fullwood Hall. Both are thought to have been medieval, single storied Hall buildings before the Tudor fashion for timbered houses came into being and both were extended upwards. Fullwood Hall later became encased in stone but Bishops' House gives an indication of how Fullwood Hall may have looked when its early Tudor occupants had completed their first modification of the earlier medieval house.

Bishops' House Meersbrook Park Sheffield

In this period, servants and farm workers are likely to have eaten in the Hall seated on benches around trestle tables. The family and any guests would sit at a table near the fire. Chairs were rare. If there were any these would be used by the adult family members and guests while the children would sit on stools. Additional seating often took the form of the great chests which were plentiful enough situated against the walls. Beds could also be used for seating. Cupboards would have stood at the far end of the Hall upon which any plate pewter or silver that the family possessed would have stood.[24]

As will be seen in the next chapter, at least one such cupboard was certainly owned by the Fox family.

It seems as though, later in the Tudor period it was decided to replace the old half-timber framed house with stone and to add a range built at right angles to the then existing house.

David Cook, in his September 2023 report also comments on this part of the Hall (and a likely later further extension) in that:

...The stonework of the walls may also be of Tudor date, though there aren't any courses of very large stones similar to the E wing. The ... datestone and the dendrochronology of some of the roof truss timbers (felled in 1618) probably represent modifications to a pre-existing building. For example, there are some timbers in the W block which are re-used or possibly in-situ. All four roof trusses have been modified ... A timber in one of them dates to 1500-25. There are also two stone fireplaces and one stone doorway thought to be of tudor date. Finally, the 1620 datestone appears to be cut in to existing courses. The range is dotted in as it exists today for context.

The writers were pleased to have confirmation that the range is also of the Tudor period which ties in with the arch and fireplaces of the same period still remaining in this part of the house. At the north-west end it appears that this range was extended over the cellars at a later date which may explain the insertion of the 1620 datestone into earlier walls.

We are, however, getting well ahead of our story, so we shall return later to the plaque above the front door of the Hall. We now go back over eighty years before the plaque was inserted into the wall, to resume the Fox family story with Robert Fox.

---

24   *See 'English Home Life 1500 – 1800' by Christina Hole for the above and much more information about how people lived in this period*

CHAPTER 4

ROBERT FOX AND SOME LATER FOXES

1537

In this year the world changed for the occupants of the substantial half-timbered, Fullwood Hall described in the previous chapter.

Fulwood had no nearby churches, the closest being in Bradfield or Hathersage. The parish church was in Sheffield, more than 5 miles away. Robert Fox is likely to have already married his wife, Emmott and had his children, William, Dorothy, and Isobel, baptised in one of these churches. However, doubt was now hanging over the old certainties concerning religious matters.

Yorkshire had always been strongly Catholic and Henry VIII's assumption of the position of Head of the Church had proved deeply unpopular. The dissolution of some of the smaller northern monasteries coupled with increased taxation to pay for the monarch's expensive foreign policy had led to the substantial uprising known as the Pilgrimage of Grace.

One of the driving forces behind the revolt was the yeomen class. This is how Robert Fox would have described himself. He and Emmott held considerable lands in Fulwood and Derbyshire, so would have been substantial and influential local figures.

It has been said of yeomen that they were only one rung on the social ladder below the gentry, and well above the bulk of the local rural population. The Reverend William Harrison writing about them in 1577 reported

"For the most part, yeomen are farmers to the gentlemen, but many are able, and do, buy the lands of unthrifty gentlemen, sending their sons to schools... or otherwise leaving them sufficient lands whereupon they may live without labor [and] by these means do make them become gentlemen"

The above is exactly what happened at Fullwood Hall, although, as will be seen, this happened some generations after the time of Robert Fox.

The historian G M Trevellyan gives us some indication of the sort of person Robert may have been:-

"As the Middle Ages drew to a close in the sixteenth century, yeomen were more numerous, wealthier, and more important than in any other age, before or after. A constant motif in the literature of the time was that the yeoman is the best type of Englishman, holding society together, neither clinging to the high, nor despising his poorer neighbours, hearty, hospitable,

and fearless. . . . . . It was a great age for the rural middle class. [25]

The Pilgrimage of Grace had only ended a few months before in nearby Doncaster. The King had met the rebel's leader at Christmas 1536 and assurances had been given that their concerns had been listened to and their demands would be met.

It is not hard to imagine therefore the nature of the conversations at Fullwood Hall in March 1537. The King had not kept his word. Beauchief Abbey was no more. It was dissolved in February 1537.

It is hard to exaggerate the importance of the Abbey to its local community. The occupants there had always been involved in their local community providing the only institutional educational and medical support for the area as well as succour for those that had fallen on hard times.

All those benefits had disappeared overnight with the dissolution of the Abbey. Robert and Emmott Fox must have felt anger and frustration, as well as fear for their family's future. The Abbey lands in Fulwood were going to be sold to noblemen who had no interest whatsoever in the local communities. The buyers might well enclose the land for their own use rather than let it to local farmers and prevent the exercise of long-established rights of common for grazing and other farming activities. It may well be that the Foxes allowed the displaced monks and lay brothers of Beauchief to have a temporary home at Fullwood Hall for a year at around this time while they were seeking a more permanent home and employment.

As if all the above was not bad enough, the harvest for 1535 had failed and rural poverty had increased in the area. The combination of likely adverse financial effects caused by the harvest failure and a time of increased taxation must have put great strain on Robert and his family. Their story will be picked up again, seven years later.

1544

Robert Fox has died. In the year before his death, he acquired a field called Benton Stubbing from John Crooke for himself and his heirs to increase their landholdings in Fulwood. Shortly afterwards he transferred this to his son.

By his will, made shortly before his death, he has requested that a Trental be performed for his soul and another for the souls of his father and mother. A Trental was a series of Masses recited by a priest at the cost of several marks[26] and which would guarantee that one's soul would be liberated from Purgatory – an early 'get out of jail free' card.

The will requested his son William and his wife Emm (also called Emmott) to share his items used for "husbandrie" during his widow's life and to share a rent to be received from Hugh Fox for a farm he was occupying at Hackenthorpe.

---

25   *G M Trevelyan English Social History. London 1944 as quoted by David B Scudder in Scudder Searches Vol v*
26   *The mark was valued at one third of a pound (6 shillings and eight pence)*

It was not a happy time. Instead of the family coming closer together there was a bitter battle being fought. The stepfamily arrangement is, even today, sometimes a difficult one and in the sixteenth century it was no different.

The mother, Emmott, had wasted little time in remarrying. She was now Mrs Edward Jackson. Before she had married Robert Fox 'of Fullwood' she had held land in Derbyshire that she had inherited from her father. Her husband, Robert Fox, had held 'diverse lands in the Parish of Sheffield,' as well as in Fulwood, so the match would have been mutually advantageous and, in the normal scheme of things, all the lands would have passed to their only son William with other provision for his two sisters, Dorothy and Isabell once both parents had died.

When Robert realized that his death was at hand, he made his will which appointed his widow Emmott sole executrix, and gave her a life interest in 'the house'. This was probably not Fullwood Hall which is more likely to have been occupied by William as the eldest son and heir. The bequest would be of another house on the Fullwood or Bradfield estate. He also made provision for his two daughters. The will did not say what was to happen should Emmott remarry.

William seems to have learned about his mother's intention of remarrying and did not take kindly to it.

Emmott's version of events is stated in a plea to the Lord Chancellor of England, Thomas Wriothesely, the 1st Earl of Southampton and the man most famous for betraying his former master Thomas Cromwell and for personally torturing Anne Askham. [27] The following is a transcription (converted into Modern English) from the plea prepared by her lawyer who described William's actions thus:-

"*Immediately after the death of the said Robert, by his effort and contrary to all right and the laws of the realm [William] did enter the home of the said Oratrix [Emmott] then being a poor widow, and did break open one cupboard of your said Oratrix from her said home where the evidence did live, and writings evidencing the Indentures of the said Oratrix did remain and such copies as the aforesaid Robert, her late husband had of the said copyhold lands, all which evidence the said William Fox did embezzle and take....... *"

The original plea is still held by the National Archives at Kew[28] and it goes on to say that William was keeping the rent from the substantial properties his father had held for himself. Unfortunately, the result of the case is not available but 'the evidence' has survived and is with the old Fullwood Hall Deeds at the Rylands library in Manchester. Young William Fox was certainly entitled to Fullwood Hall as the eldest son, so it may be that the application was really being instigated by Edward Jackson, the new husband as the plea only asks for the documents taken to be produced. This may indicate that he is 'fishing' to see if can get his hands on any entitlement his wife had in respect of the lands that were previously hers before her first marriage. In the normal course of events these would have passed to her first husband and it may well be that they were assigned to William during Robert's lifetime, or automatically on his death, as a will only dealt with the personal estate of the deceased. It is significant that the plea does not claim that Emmott had any

27   *The National Archives at Kew hold her petition ref Jackson v Foxe C1/1134/29*

28   *Jacksone v Foxe Chancery etc 1544-1551 Ref C1/1134/29*

entitlement and even says that she does not know what the deeds and documents may contain.

Later Fox occupants of Fullwood Hall certainly had the benefit of land both in Fulwood and Bradfield in Derbyshire and it is quite possible that some of the combined estates were acquired through the marriage of Robert and Emmott Fox. It is certain that William Fox died at Fullwood Hall in 1580. This is almost certain to have been the cupboard-breaking and deed-taking young man of 1544.

There is an interesting entry in the Court Rolls for Sheffield that may relate to this William Fox.

23rd June 1550

Robert Beighton surrenders to William Fox one dole of land in Okenall, also a parcel of Le Appleyard adjoining the Brode Croft belonging to the said William, a house–close called le Farfeild, a croft called le brodecroft, a close called Woodlouse adjoining le Snathynglowe and a third part of the pasturage for 5 beasts in the field of Hallam and the said William Fox to have sufficient road with his carriages over land of Robert Beghton called Hollyngflatt. Fee of 4d to the Lord of the Manor.

Given how often the name Okenall (or some variation thereof) appears in connection with the Fullwood Hall Foxes, it is very likely that this is the same William, the son of Robert and Emmot Fox. The Fox family continued to own fields in Hallam until the late 1690's.

Little else is known of this William other than through the contents of his will and that of his wife Margaret both of which have survived and are held in the Borthwick Institute in York[29]. William died in 1580, but Margaret, his wife, remained living in Fullwood until her death in 1597. They both benefitted their many children. William's eldest son inherited the Hall but he was requested to allow his nine siblings to have their share of the barley and other grasses growing in the fields and half of the manure at the Hall and use of the horses until the next feast of St Phillip and St James! William described himself as a yeoman and, at least two of his sons were still young as money was set aside to pay for the 'growing up in learning' of his son Edward, and for his tuition and maintenance as well as that of his brother John. William was unusual in providing for his sons' education as schooling would not be considered important for most farming families in the region at this time.

It seems that William owned armour as he left the harness to protect his horse to his son, William. Sixteen years later, Margaret leaves several beds, bedding, and household items to her children. Intriguingly she benefits the same children as had her husband, William, but she also makes a gift to 'her daughter' an extra child called Grace who she says is already married and now called Grace Hobson. She has not had time to have another child of marriageable age after the death of her husband so it is likely that Grace was born from a previous relationship and that Margaret was a widow when she married into the Fox family. She may have been of the local Greaves family as she makes her cousin, Richard Greaves one of the Supervisors of her will.

---

29   Borthwick Institute York William's 6th July 1580 Will Proved 8th Sept 1580 (Vol 21 fol: 407)
     Margarets 16th November 1596 Will Proved 13th April 1597 (Vol 26 fol: 510)

It is probably not significant that Margaret makes no provision for the eldest son, William, or his children (although she benefits all the other children and grandchildren). William's branch of the family had already inherited the Hall so she may have felt that they were already well provided for. Relations between Margaret and her son were cordial enough as she made him one of the witnesses of her Will and presumably he called his first-born child, Margaret, after her.

The story will resume with Margaret's son, William Fox (Junior), living at the Hall.

1591

The younger William had moved to Fullwood Hall and started a family by 1591. At that time, he must have been one of the most respected men in the neighbourhood. In the previous year he had brought an action jointly with Robert Mitchell of Stumperlowe against the Lord of the Manor of Sheffield on a matter of vital importance to those living in the whole region.

In a little before the year 1300, Thomas Furnival, the then Lord of Hallamshire, gave a charter to all the men of Stannington, Morewood, Hallam and Fullwood for rights of herbage and foliage throughout:

'The whole of his forest of Riveling as it lies in length and breadth between Malin Bridge, Belhag and Whitely Wood of the one part and a place called Stanedge and the common way which leads from Sheffield towards Derwent on the other.'

For these collective rights the sum of £4 of silver was payable annually to the Lord of the Manor of Sheffield, in later years this was being paid as to £2 by the tenants in Stannington and as to the other £2 by the Upper Hallam tenants and to which William would have contributed his share. These rights do not sound much today, but then they were vital for the profitable running of any farm as they included the ability to let their livestock graze and to collect wood for fuel, thatching and other purposes.

The importance of these rights is indicated by some of the fines that were imposed on 'outsiders' who tried to muscle in on the Rivelin commoners' rights. The following are contained in the Sheffield Manor Court Rolls and the large amounts are indicative of how valuable those rights and the maintenance of those woods and commons were to those living in Fulwood. Listed below are just a few of the penalties to be faced by outsiders:

For any person putting cattle on the common of Reivelin Wood who is not an inhabitant of the liberty of Stannington, Moorwood, Hallam or Fullwood, a fine of £1 19s 11d

For gathering dung from the common 6s 8d

For putting scabbed horses on the Common £1 13s 4d

William Fox and Robert Mitchell will have made themselves popular with the local inhabitants as their application was successful and the Court Rolls for the year 30 Elizabeth (1589) show that they obtained 'exemplification' of the ancient Charter thereby frustrating the Lord of the Manor's attempt to use the land for just his own purposes.

Taking on such a powerful opponent will have required courage and someone who was prepared to challenge supposed social superiors. William is described in the Court Rolls as a yeoman but it seems that he was not the usual type of farmer. He had given his children unusual names taken from early civilizations. Not many gave their children names like Sophronia, Gertrude, or Zacharias, yet alone Ulysses. Even the names Rosemary, Sarah and Judith were relatively uncommon, and Margaret was, no doubt, named in honour of his mother yet those are the names William chose for his children.

The choice of names may also show an attempt by William Fox to emphasize his status. Fullwood Hall was already a substantial building and it is probably he who was responsible for new building work and the typically Tudor doorways and fireplaces inside the building as well as being the owner of the stone table which was possibly taken from Beauchief Abbey following its dissolution, and a little over fifty years later, described as an 'heirloom' standing in the Hall parlour.

From William's own will dated 1609 we know that his wife was called Joanne. [30] He leaves his musket to his son Ulysses; he also gives him all the glass in the window of his chamber and in the parlour at the Hall. Glass ownership indicates how the family fortunes had improved during William's lifetime. Shortly the Hall itself would receive a new extension. However, that would be carried out by William's son Ulysses, who will be met in the next chapter.

---

30   *Borthwick Institute York. Will dated 21ˢᵗ September 1609. Proved 1ˢᵗ October 1612 (Vol 32 Folio 169)*

CHAPTER 5

ULYSSES FOX

1620

Ulysses Fox was baptized at Royston (near Barnsley) on 14th Feb 1575/6. Three of his sisters were also baptized there so it seems that they were brought up in Royston until their parents were able to move to Fullwood Hall after the death of William Fox in 1580. On 3rd November 1612, Ulysses appeared at the Lord of the Manor's Court where he was acknowledged son and heir of his father William Fox. He therefore became entitled to *"one messuage and half an oxgang of land Hastler and one third of an oxgang of land Hastler in Fullwood of which the yearly rent to the Lord was ix s x d and a halfpenny (9s 10 ½ d) and one close called Benton Stubbings in Fullwood of which the yearly rent to the Lord was xiid (one shilling)"*

Benton Stubbings had been acquired for the family by Robert Fox in 1543 and the rest of the land has a similar description to that inherited by Agnes, the wife of John Fox way back in 1428. The 'messuage' mentioned was the family house in Fulwood which was shortly to undergo some renovation. Like his father, William, Ulysses was not afraid of taking on authority. He also liked to put on a show. Others in the neighbourhood were building, or extending, their homes [31] and Ulysses was planning to do the same. He had married a well-connected girl from Bradfield who brought with her a substantial dowry. Elizabeth Greene was the daughter of William Greene, the Bailiff of Bradfield, and a substantial landowner there. The connection would bring considerable wealth into the Fox family. In 1618 Ulysses and Elizabeth had given her father, the wealthy William Greene, a male heir. He was called William Fox and was just two-years old in 1620.

Building work had begun at Fullwood Hall, which was to have a new extension to the frontage, projecting outwards from the north west end of the house. The projection was built directly above the cellar. It would have its own roof, at a different level to the range, and impressive mullioned windows to match those that already existed. The new works will have created a much more impressive-looking building that would be a distinguished home for the newly-married couple and their family. It is possible that the front door was replaced, well above which a plaque was inserted set into existing courses of stone. This both commemorated the marriage and showed who had caused such an impressively fronted building to be created. The plaque was to bear the initials V, E and F and the date 1620.

V was a traditional way of depicting U in those days so the initials were to represent the Christian names Ulysses (usually spelt Ulisses in official records) and Elizabeth. The F denoted their surname of Fox.

---

31   *As happened at Whirlow and Stumperlowe*

Original Building, range and new extension- illustration by Alan Crutch

The new frontage is shown in the centre of the painting. The main part and the unseen area behind the new projection is the range, and the oldest part of the house is the building to the right, at a right angle to the rest of the Hall, and with a lower roof.

Tudor interior doorway and bedroom fireplace with "Humped" lintels

Inside the Hall, behind the new extension and within the range, are tantalising signs of the pre-1620 house as then occupied by Ulysses and his family, but which previously would have been part of his parents and grandparents' home.

Old Kitchen Tudor fireplace with "Humped" lintel

As well as the doorway and fireplaces with their 'humped' arches, there are many old timber beams that show evidence of witch-marks (more correctly called apotropaic marks). It is not known when they may have been carved or scratched into the beams but, in the sixteenth and early seventeenth centuries there was a considerable popular fear of the power of witchcraft. It was thought that evil could be confused by, turned away, or trapped within the graffiti so any malevolent forces would be powerless to have any effect upon the occupants. The dendro-chronology report, commissioned in 2023, indicated that one roof timber has a last growth ring in 1482, and another in 1488. Allowing for the removed sapwood rings (varying between 15 and 40 and a ring for each year missing as the time when these timbers formed part of the Hall roof.

Were the marks on the timbers made by the roofers, Ulysses himself, or by one of his predecessors? It is, of course, impossible to tell but whoever it was would have had to stand on a ladder or table with one hand holding a candlestick to have enough light to work by.

It is impossible for us now to understand the meaning of the marks, but the overlapping circles carved into one of the Hall beams have been identified in old houses elsewhere. [32] At Fullwood Hall they appear in what is thought to be the oldest part of the house. In other contexts, and throughout the ages, circles have been used as a symbol of continuity and completeness. Was a new circle added by each successor when they moved into the Hall or was a new one carved for every child born to one branch of the family? The answer is one of the many secrets the Hall keeps to itself.

---

32   *For a similar set of symbols see https://historicengland.org.uk/whats-new/features/discovering-witches-marks/types-of-marks/*

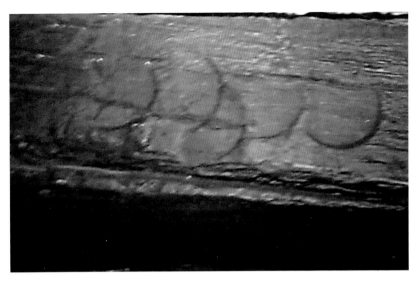

Overlapping circles on beam

As well as those shown above, the circle motif appears quite regularly on the downstairs Hall beams, but neither do they always overlap nor are they always perfect circles, as can be seen from the next illustration.

More circles

There are also several 'burn' marks in the roof timbers. These were deliberately created with a candle or poker and are thought to have been done to give the house protection against fire and lightning. Below is a good example.

A number of roof timbers have carpenters' marks including the Union Jack and the St Andrew's flags and, almost wherever you look there are strange marks.

Burn mark on Window lintel timber

Other timber marks

By the time the work was finished the outside appearance of Fullwood Hall will have been much as it is today, complete with the plaque already described. Ulysses and Elizabeth raised their four children there and they will all have lived in one of the most prestigious buildings in their neighbourhood. This was a time when the power and influence of the Fullwood Hall estate was still growing.

What happened afterwards forms the next part of the story but before concluding this section it is only fitting that we should leave with the most visible personal memorial to Ulysses and Elizabeth Fox, the plaque that still can be seen above the front door of Fullwood Hall.

Plaque

1649

Ulysses Fox has died. He was named after the Greek hero, Odysseus. Ulysses was his Roman name. Like the Greek hero himself, and like Robert and the William Foxes before him, he had lived in eventful times. He was born in the year that the Spanish Armada set sail, lived through the Gunpowder Plot of 1605 as well as the English Civil War and died in the same year that Charles I was beheaded. Like his father he had confronted authority head-on by constructing water mills just down the road from Fullwood Hall. This enabled those in the locality to have their corn ground locally rather than travel many miles to the Lord of the Manor's mill several miles away. In those days the Lord had a monopoly so Ulysses was obliged to pay the Lord what was likely to have been an eventually agreed sum (described as a 'Fine') of £35 8s 9d. The mills remained in the family until the end of the seventeenth century, and served the local community for over two hundred years.

Elizabeth, Ulysses' wife, had died in 1536, and her wealthy father, William Greene, also died shortly afterwards. George Fox, Ulysses and Elizabeth's eldest grandson and William's great grandson would stand to inherit all his great-grandfather's possessions. William Greene's will shows his family home was in Smallfield in Bradfield. He also owned a farm and land in Killamarsh and was entitled to tithes and other payments due in respect of the parsonage at Bradfield. All these were given to the Fox family. Initially they will have gone to George's father William Fox but on his death in 1648 the whole estate passed to young George Fox. Young George was also the heir to all Ulysses Fox estate so Fullwood Hall would also become George's once he reached the then distant age of twenty-one years.

We are fortunate that court records concerning George still exist. [33] The case brought by George in 1689 shows that his Father William was living with his young wife, Ann, and family at Fullwood Hall at the time of William's death in 1648. William had been aged only 30 when he died but had made a good marriage into another landowning local family. His wife was Anne Morewood whose family lived at 'the Oaks' in Bradfield.

Anne and William already had six children. The eldest was George Fox, but he was only six years old.

William Fox is reported to have been a Major in the Yorkshire contingent of the Parliamentary army in the civil war[34], His death occurred during those years and it may well be that such an early death was a result of wounds received in that conflict. It may be significant that he received armour from William Greene, his maternal grandfather.

So, by 1649, William is dead and his heir is very young. We will return to what happens to young George later, but first we need to finish the story of Ulysses Fox, the real subject of this chapter.

As well as William, another of Ulysses' sons, George, had died in 1648 so Ulysses had to set his mind, very rapidly, to what should happen to his estate after his death. He had already completed deeds that had placed the ownership of Fullwood Hall in the hands of his eldest remaining son William and his heirs. He had also allowed his son Stephen to occupy the farm in Hackenthorpe and his son John to take the one at High Storrs. By his Will dated 14th October 1648 he gave the deeds of those properties to Stephen and John. He also made several gifts to the poor of Sheffield, Hallam and Ecclesall and gives 20 shillings for a" a good preacher" to conduct a suitable memorial service at his funeral. He also left two Spurr Ryalls to his cousin Ann Hill of Sheffield. A Spurr Royal was a gold coin worth 15 shillings each then. Now they are excessively rare and one would fetch over £30,000!

The will contains information about the Hall and an indication of a scandal that may have happened there. He gives the stone table around which legend still exists, that was standing in the Great Parlour at Fullwood Hall, to his son's widow Anne but then changes his mind at the end of the will and gives it, together with its stand, to her son, his grandson, George Fox.

In addition to other gifts, he leaves 20 shillings to his ex-apprentice William Fox (as if one with that name was not bad enough)

What really stands out in the will is the gift to his servant, Ann Ryles. She receives the enormous sum of three pounds and "the bed in which she lyeth" Those with a suspicious mind may well be considering exactly what services she was supplying to Ulysses (who had been a widow for over 10 years.) Well, if you do think that you are wrong. There was indeed a sexual connection , but it was not with Ulysses. The Sheffield Parish Register shows that on 13th February 1636/7 Ann Ryles' son John was christened after being born illegitimate and that the putative father was named as William Fox, presumably the son rather than the ex-apprentice! In 1648

33   Foxe v Bulguy held by the National Archives under reference c 6/263/51 (1689)
34   The Cromwell Association. Online Directory of Parliamentary Officers – Published by British History Online 2017

when the will was written, Ann Ryles was still in service, but had been shipped out with her son John to High Storrs where, Ulysses' own son John was living. It is not unreasonable to think that the conception may have been at Fullwood Hall and that the teenager William had felt the sharp end of his father's tongue as a direct result.

An eldest son making a servant girl pregnant at the Hall is a theme that will be returned to a little more than fifty years later, but first there follows a brief summary of what young George would stand to inherit as the eldest son of an eldest son, following the deaths of both his father and his grandfather.

The land holdings had been extended by the purchase of the Broad and Daw fields from Lawrence Hall and his son, the then owners of Bennet Grange. The family also owned a property known as Ewe House where it seems Ulysses was living at the time of that purchase. In the case already mentioned it is clearly stated that there were also 'messuages and tenements' situate as part of the estate and near to Fullwood Hall.

As already mentioned, the Foxes already owned land in Bradfield, going back to the days of Robert and Emmott Fox. These holdings were greatly increased by the will of William Greene dated just after his daughter, Ulysses Fox's wife Elizabeth Fox's death in 1636.

The personal possessions given were:-

"I give and bequeath unto Ulisses ffox my sonne in law my best horse or mare with the furniture to the same belonging in such sorte as I am wont to use in ridinge" and

"I give unto William ffox my grandchild all my books. My greatest peece my crossbowe and sack and my best hanger all my armour of warr w'th a shorte arming sword to the same belonging"

Although the gift of armour sounds anachronistic it did still have a use as the Harrison survey of 1637 stated that William Fox was obliged to provide a horse to be part of the parade at Sembley Green in Sheffield on Easter Tuesday. This pageant harked back to the days when the holders of ancient lands had to provide their Lord with military services, so dressing in armour would be the correct dress for the occasion. William will have used this for the years after William Greene's death in 1640. It may well be that William wore it in his role as a Major in the Civil War. It will all have formed part of his son, George Fox's inheritance.

William Greene's will relates that he had already given a lease to the Fox family, to take effect on his death, of the rectory or parsonage at Bradfield with an entitlement to a share of the tithes due from the tenants which included:-

'One halfpenny for every lamb fallen within the said property or sold out of it between lambing time and clipping time'

The lease was stated to be for the benefit of Ulysses Fox's children and at the end of the lease the entitlement was to revert to William Fox and his heirs. The value of all the property that would come to the very young George Fox was later stated to be worth the extremely large amount of two hundred and fifty pounds a year.

In 1637 there had been a comprehensive survey of lands in the Manor of Sheffield carried out by John Harrison which shows how extensive the Fox lands of this period were. Ulysses Fox was paying 10s 6d a year to the Lord of the Manor by way of rent for some land forming part of the Estate and a further sum as rent for a holly hagg with which to feed his sheep in winter. The fact that many ordinary tenants in the region had their holdings defined by their whereabouts in relation to land of Ulysses Fox indicates that his holdings were more secure than those of the ordinary tenants of the Lord of the Manor, and from the various field descriptions it is possible to gain hints of some of the land that was part of the Fox estate at this time. As well as Broad Field and Daw Field that he had purchased from the Lawrence Halls, it is likely that he owned the other fields adjacent to the Hall as well as the Oakney fields above the Hall. He also owned three fields to the East of the Oakneys, in the Crimicar Lane area, known as Hallom Fields as well as the mills in Fulwood and the other houses and tenements near Fullwood Hall.

George Fox would be a very wealthy young man if he lived to reach the age of twenty-one. The next chapter will see him as a young man, married and living with his wife in Fullwood Hall.

The gift to George Fox of the stone table in the codicil to the will is shown below together with a transcription.

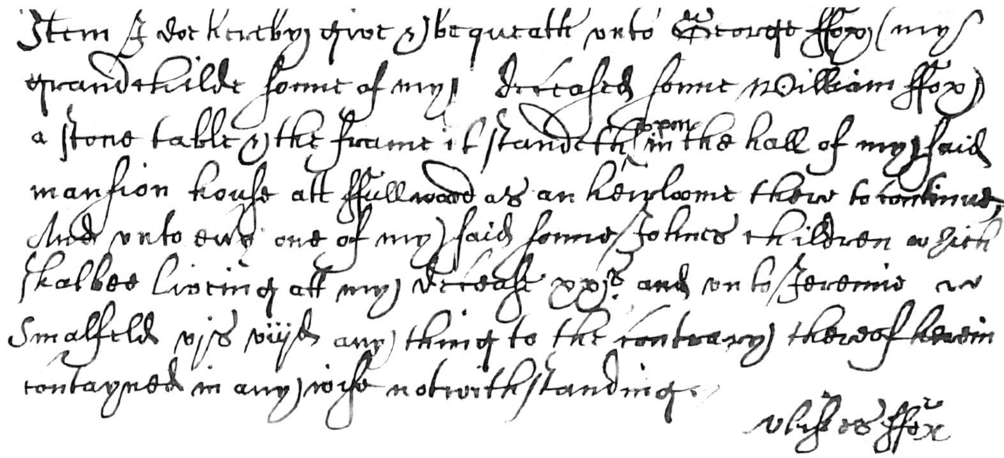

Codicil to the 1648 will of Ulysses Fox

> *Item I doe hereby give & bequeath unto George ffox (my*
> *grandchilde sonne of my deceased sonne William ffox)*
> *a stone table & the frame it standeth /upon/ in the hall of my said*
> *mansion house att ffullwood as an heirloome there to continue*
> *And unto ev'ry one of my said sonne Johnes children which*
> *shal bee living at my decease XX s (£1) and unto Jeremie*
> *Smalfeld vi s viii d[35] any thing to the contrary thereof herein*
> *contayned in any wise notwithstandinge*
> *Ulisses ffox*

---

35 6s 8d one third of £1 - known as a Mark. Extract provided with the kind permission of the Borthwick Institute York.

"View from the Hall fields across the Mayfield Valley" a painting by Caroline Holley

CHAPTER 6

GEORGE FOX

1666

George Fox, the son of William and Anne Fox is Lord and master of Fullwood Hall. He has already adopted the title of 'Gentleman'. The first of his family living at Fullwood Hall to do so. He has just married Dorothy Balgay, the daughter of a family wealthy enough to provide a dowry of £500. They have moved into Fullwood Hall where they intend to raise a family to take on the Fox dynasty.

This young George Fox has a rather unusual claim to fame in that his grandfather was also his step-father. This strange situation arose as a result of Henry Balgay, his wife's father, taking William's widowed mother, Anne, as his third wife. George records what happened following the death of his mother in the court case brought against Henry Balgay's son, also called Henry. [36]

During George's minority Fullwood Hall had not been his home. At the time of his marriage settlement dated 1st November 1665, his address was given as 'Smallfield' the home of his grandmother, the old Greene family residence. He had been living there with his mother and, presumably, his younger siblings. Fullwood Hall and all the other properties that George would receive were managed by his new step-father Henry Balgay.

There follows a very much-abridged family tree of George Fox. A more detailed family tree is reproduced in Appendix 2.

The illustration highlights George's descent from Robert and Emmott Fox, through William and Margaret Fox and then Ulysses and Elizabeth, and his own parents, William, and Anne, It also shows his relationship to John and Stephen Fox, his father's brothers, and the Executors of their wills and possibly most importantly to his story, his relationship with Henry Balgay.

---

36   *Fox v Balguy 1689 case already described*

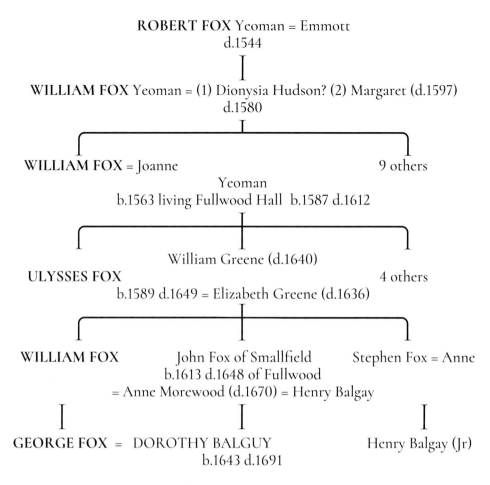

ROBERT FOX Yeoman = Emmott
d.1544

WILLIAM FOX Yeoman = (1) Dionysia Hudson? (2) Margaret (d.1597)
d.1580

WILLIAM FOX = Joanne   9 others
Yeoman
b.1563 living Fullwood Hall b.1587 d.1612

William Greene (d.1640)
ULYSSES FOX   4 others
b.1589 d.1649 = Elizabeth Greene (d.1636)

WILLIAM FOX   John Fox of Smallfield   Stephen Fox = Anne
b.1613 d.1648 of Fullwood
= Anne Morewood (d.1670) = Henry Balgay

GEORGE FOX = DOROTHY BALGUY   Henry Balgay (Jr)
b.1643 d.1691

Table 1 ancestors of George Fox

The 1689 case shows how important Henry Balgay was to George Fox. George relates that his widowed mother, Ann, married Henry Balgay, and that according to George, Henry Balgay

"took upon him the tuition and management of his Estate for eleaven yeares and upwards"

Towards the end of the eleven years George says that he was encouraged to marry one of Henry's daughters by a previous marriage and he duly married Dorothy Balgay once he had reached the age of 21 years.

After the marriage George continued to depend on Henry Balguy. George's lawyer says of him that Henry

"exprest soe great kindnesse and respect (to George) and was soe ready to assist and advise (George) in the ordering and managing his Estate that he (George) was wholly governed and controlled by him in his affairs"

Henry Balgay had therefore been responsible for Fullwood Hall during unprecedented times. There was no monarch from 1649 until 1660. The Commonwealth and Protectorate had been a time of the Major Generals and taxation to maintain the army had been exorbitant, particularly for those who had taken up the Royalist cause during the civil war. It seems that William Fox chose the Parliamentary side but it is not known which side the rest of the Fox family supported. Sheffield had been ambivalent about which side it supported. Sometimes Sheffield Castle was in the King's hands, sometimes the Parliamentarians had control. Although William Fox may have been a Major with the 'Roundheads' it is quite possible that his father, Ulysses, may have been a Royalist sympathizer. Quite a few families hedged their bets in that way.

An intriguing find in the garden of Fullwood Hall is a small, iron cannonball that probably dates from that period. It is certainly possible that a forge at the Hall was being used to make shot for cannons.

When the war ended with the execution of the King, in 1649, it was still a capital offense to administer the Catholic Mass, so, if it was still being celebrated at Fullwood Hall by whoever was living there at that time, the signals sent from Priest Hill mentioned earlier would have been needed. Given the inherent Catholic sentiment in Yorkshire at this time it is certainly possible that priests may have made regular visits to Fullwood Hall and the legend of a tunnel or passage from Fullwood Hall to Bennett Grange possibly originated in this period.

Given the level of taxation during the Commonwealth period, it may be that Henry Balgay, on behalf of the young George Fox, had to be pragmatic and accept what income he could get from Fullwood Hall and if it came from Catholics they could always have claimed not to know. Alternatively, the Fox or Balgay families may well have had Catholic sympathies themselves and welcomed priests to a remote, out of the way, place where they might administer to those of the old faith still living in the area, yet escape in the times when there might be Pursuivants searching for Catholic priests in the area, after they had received the advance warning from Priest Hill.

By 1666, the year of the great fire of London. the monarchy had been restored, and the Catholic sympathizing Stuarts were now back on the throne. The repressive days of the Commonwealth were over and enjoyment (often to excess) was the new expectation for many young men. The extent to which this applied to young George Fox and his family will shortly be seen. First though we need to look ahead only ten years.

1676

Yet again we find ourselves in a year when tragedy had returned to Fullwood Hall. Dorothy has died giving birth to her sixth child. Her first child Henry had died in infancy and maybe calling her last child Henry was a bad omen. Muriel Hall, quoting Colin Cooper, sums up the atmosphere of the time,

"What a sad day that was for Henry's baptism on 16th August 1676. Only five days earlier, a mournful procession left Fullwood Hall carrying across the Moors the mortal remains of his mother who had died, aged thirty-three years, leaving George Fox with five children under nine years of age. She was buried, not in the soft, gentle valley churchyard at Hope

with her ancestors, but high up on the rugged hillside at Bradfield, not far from the grave of her husband's great grandfather, William Greene, from whom had come the Fox Bradfield estates."

As well as baby Henry. George was left with two other sons William (b 1668) and George (b 1670) aged 8 and 6 respectively as well as two daughters, Anne and Elizabeth aged 4 and 2. George will have relied on his mother's family the Balgays for help but it is hardly surprising that his mind had already turned to remarriage.

As already described, George Fox was a wealthy man. The Hearth Tax returns for 1672 provide a snapshot of the sort of houses owned by George Fox at that time and the sizes of the communities in which his family lived.

As indicated by the name, the tax was based on the number of hearths (fireplaces with chimneys) that any individual house possessed.

Fullwood Hall is unique in that it appears in the return for Upper Hallam under its own name rather than under the name of the owner. Of the 86 houses listed in the whole of Upper Hallam, only 3 had more than 5 hearths. Fullwood Hall had 7.

In 1672 the owner (at least in as far as being just a life tenant) was George Fox but his name does not appear in the record for Upper Hallam. William Fox owned 2 houses there, one with only one hearth and the other with two. One of the Fox widows lived in another small house and Georges' uncle, Stephen Fox, also lived locally in a more modest house with two hearths.

The return for Bradfield parish shows many similarities to that of Upper Hallam. Next to the name 'Mr Fox' (presumably George Fox) is listed a house with 5 hearths. This will have been the house in Smallfield originally owned by Ulysses Fox's wife's family. Again, it is one of the three largest houses in the parish. Mr Fox, gentleman, also owned a house with 4 hearths in the Bradfield parish of Westnall. This is likely to have been More Hall. Only a select few in the returns are described as 'Mr.' That title was reserved only for gentlemen. This is proof that even at the age of 29 George Fox was recognized as a member of that very select group. On the basis that the properties he owned had 16 hearths between them, George will have had to pay £1 16s 0d a year for the privilege. There is a further entry for a George Fox in Sheffield for a property that had 4 hearths and an extra one for a forge, but there is no direct evidence to connect that George Fox to the owner of Fullwood Hall although one of George's sons is later recorded as operating a pottery on the site of Sheffield Manor.

Despite all this wealth, there was a considerable disadvantage for any new intended bride's family considering a match, in that George already had an heir (and two spares!) and, in any event, only held a life interest in most of his property[37]. This meant that there was little chance of any children he might have with a new wife inheriting George's Estate. It may therefore explain why George's choice of a new wife would fall on the daughter of a very wealthy and influential, but staunchly Catholic, family, the Poles (or Pooles) from Park Hall, Barlborough. That family did not need George's inheritance. They will have wanted to ensure that their daughter lived comfortably in the home of a gentleman. There were three Pole daughters, but George's choice was to marry Mary Pole and the marriage would take place in the

---

37   *Fox v Balguy 1689 again*

church at Barlborough in 1679.

George had already decided to adopt a Coat of Arms for himself. It was a bear carrying an axe with the motto 'And Let God Help'[38] In his choice of bride it might well be argued that God must have guided his choice, as will appear later. The Coat of Arms was never formally registered but does appear in a downstairs window of the Hall. One of those put in by George's grandfather Ulysses. If the Arms were displayed in the window at that time, it would show an earlier use of them by the Fox family. The present owner of the Hall, Roger Hostombe has formally adopted the bear with an axe as part of his registered Coat of Arms.

George Fox's unofficial coat of arms in Hall window

By 1676 it is likely that George Fox had forged friendships with two other young men. Henry Hall of Stumperlowe Hall and Henry Bright of Whirlow Hall. These were all young men with bright prospects and it is reported that they used to meet at a small establishment just down the road from Fullwood Hall named Water Carr Hall. The outcome of these connections will become clearer later in the story.

---

38 *For subsequent use of the Coat of Arms please see Chapter 19*

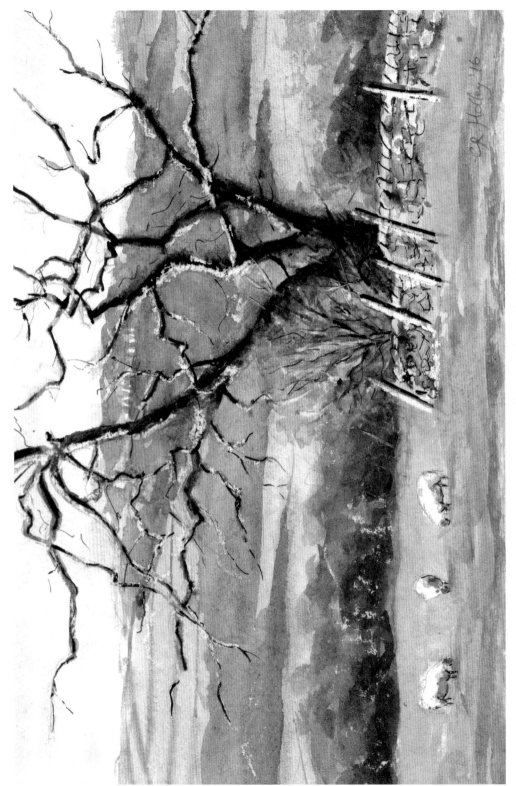

"Sheep Grazing on Daw Field" painting by Caroline Holley

UNDER PRESSURE

1690

George Fox is still living at Fullwood Hall with Mary who has just given birth to their 5th child, a girl also called Mary. Their other children are all boys, Frances, James, John, and Michael aged nine, eight, six, and three respectively. They have all been brought up in the Catholic faith. The children of George's first marriage had been raised as Protestants. The son and heir, William, is now a young man and regularly joins his father at Water Carr Hall. William is living at Ewes House, the same address as that given by his great grandfather Ulysses back in 1622. William has just signed a deed confirming the sale of More Hall by his father George where his address is given as Ewes House. Both had to sign as George only had a life interest and William had to confirm that he would have no claim on More Hall when his father died.

More Hall had, and still has, some renown. The hero of the tale of 'The Dragon of Wantley' is reputed to have lived there. The poem had been published in 1685 in a collection of tales known as 'Broadside Ballads'[39]. In the tale, More, of More Hall, saved the local inhabitants by bespeaking a special suit of armour from Sheffield town completely covered in long spikes between five and six inches long. Dressed in this armour he killed the dragon by kicking it in its only vulnerable, and painful, spot. Before this, he had been 'anointed,' overnight, by a young maiden and then, to fortify himself for the fight, he drank six pots of ale and a quart of aqua-vitae. He hid in a well and leapt out when the dragon came to drink.

The ballad later became a comic opera performed in Covent Garden in London. Did George have anything to do with the publication of the ballad in 1685? It is impossible to say, but it is certainly the sort of bawdy, comic, heroic tale that would have appealed to a gentleman as convivial as George. It is quite possible to imagine him drinking with his friends from Whirlow and Stumperlowe Halls and entertaining them with this ballad at Water Carr Hall.

The fact that George and William have just sold More Hall indicates that there are financial problems. Certainly, all is not well between George Fox and his friend at Stumperlowe Hall. In Colin Cooper's notes about Fullwood Hall, there is a copy of a letter written in George Fox's own hand. It is a brief, and to the point, letter demanding repayment of money owed. The letter is reproduced here, followed by the writer's transcription, but first a little background to show a financial connection between the two families.

Back in 1677 and 1678 the records of the Burgesses of Sheffield show that George Fox and Robert Hall were lent a total of £70 by the Town Trustees of Sheffield in return for a bond whereby George and Robert agreed to repay the same, with

---

39   *A True Relation of the Dreadful Combat between More of More Hall and the Dragon of Wantley' Broadside Ballads published by Randall Taylor. London. 1685.*

interest. At around the same time George signed a similar bond borrowing £50 jointly with Henry Balguy, his wife's father and mother's husband.[40] These were large amounts for those times. By 1690 the amount owing on the Fox/Balguy bond was £19 3s 2d and the amount due under the Fox/Hall bond was £27 4s 0d. Both debts were fully repaid before or very shortly after George's death It is possible that the following letter relates to promised repayment by the Hall family in respect of their share of what was due under their bond. The dealings between George and Henry Balguy are already mired in litigation. [41]

The Town Trustees accounts show payment for a messenger being sent, at this time, to both George Fox and Robert Hall with a request to make some repayment under their Bond. Maybe that was what prompted the writing of the following letter, the original of which is housed in the Barnsley Archives. Its survival is because it was found in a pocket almanac belonging to the recipient Henry Hall.

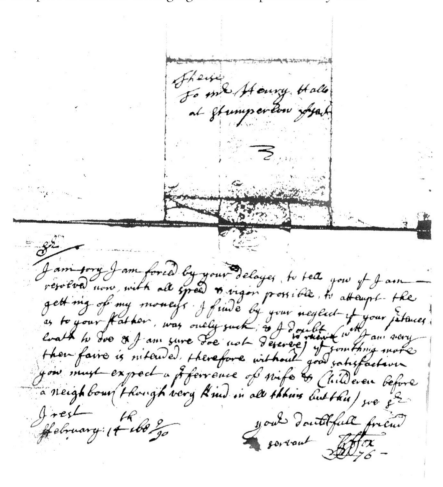

Letter. George Fox to Henry Hall[42]

40   There were two Henry Balguys alive at this time. Both figure prominently in the Fox history. One was Georges first wives' father and the other her brother and Henry's son

41   National Archives Fox v Balguy Ref C6/412/76

42   Reproduced by courtesy of Barnsley Archives,.

It reads:-

These
To Mr Henry Hall
At Stumperlow

Sir
I am sor(r)y I am fo(r)ced by your delayes, to tell you t(hat) I am
resolved now, with all speed & vigour possible, to attempt the
getting of my monies. I finde by your neglect t(hat) your p(r)etence
as to your father, was only such: & I doubt (w(hi)chi I am very loathe
to doe & I am sure doe not deserve to receive t(hat) something more
than faire is intended, therefore without good satisfaction
you must expect a p(re)ference of wife & Children before
a neighbour (although very kind in all things but this) soe t(hus)
I rest
February 14th 1689/9043   *Your doubtful friend*
                                 And servant G ffox

It is unlikely that George received satisfaction, as requested, but this was far from the only concern that he must have had at this time. His mentor Henry Balguy had died, and Henry's son was much less indulgent of George Fox than his father had been. The younger Henry was his father's Executor and was in a difficult position. His father, the elder Henry, had left monetary gifts to Mary, the second wife of George, and their children. He also left larger sums to his own Fox grandchildren, the children of George Fox and Dorothy Balgay. Before those gifts were taken into consideration Henry the Executor claimed that George Fox owed his father Henry the stupendous sum of £2,500, and after the value of the gifts was deducted, because he felt George should pay them, the Executor, Henry, maintained that this still left George Fox owing the Estate over £2,000. Because of the alleged debt Henry had issued proceedings in the Kings Bench for the whole Fullwood Estate to be forfeited by George in favour of the Executor, Henry Balguy[44]. George had applied for equitable relief denying any debt and claiming that the elder Henry had been a Trustee and that the Trust obligations should be passed on to Henry the Executor. The details of the case are interesting but very technical and ultimately not relevant to the ownership of Fullwood Hall for reasons that will be later explained

The case records that Henry Balgay had acted in a case against George Fox on behalf of Henry Eyre and obtained a verdict from Derby Assizes whereby George's lands in Derbyshire should be given to Henry Eyre. There was also a further ongoing case in Yorkshire that Henry Balguy was prosecuting. Things were certainly looking bleak for George Fox and it seems that he was on the verge of losing everything as the year 1690 drew to an unhappy close.

Ultimately however, George did not have to repay anything nor did his family lose their land and estates or have to pay George's debts. Neither Henry Balgay in his own capacity as Executor of his father's will nor any of his clients received anything.

---

43   *The 1689/90 date is because the new year did not begin until 25th March at that time*
44   *As reported in Fox v Balguy*

It cannot though be said that George Fox had won. Rather ironically, the old Henry Balgay who it will be remembered was both step-father and father-in-law to George was the family's saviour in this respect.

George avoided all his responsibilities by the simple expedient of his own death in the summer of 1691. In his lifetime he had complained bitterly that Henry Balgay as his wife-to-be's father had insisted that George Fox's interest in all the property he had inherited from his father should be reduced to just a life interest with everything going to George and Dorothy's eldest male child on George's death, yet this arrangement very neatly frustrated all claims against George including those of Henry Balgay's own son. On death all George's land passed on to his son William Fox free of all debt and it is very unlikely that George had much in the way of personal assets to set against what seems to be debts running well into thousands of pounds if the younger Henry Balgay's statement in his own case is to be believed.

George Fox was buried at Sheffield Parish Church on 3rd August 1691. Did the financial pressures he was under directly cause or contribute to his death? Henry Hall, the recipient of the letter claiming repayment of money due from the Hall family, died in the following February. Henry Balgay's claim needs to be seen in the light of the fact that the Balgays seem to have been very litigious as evidenced by the number of cases that are held in the National Archives for this period. Henry does say that his father provided money to pay out one obligation that George certainly had, as it was contained in George's father's will. It was that George had to pay out £250 to each of his siblings on them respectively attaining the age of 21 years. As his siblings were all a similar age to George this would have been a substantial liability and it is certainly very likely that George turned to his father-in-law to lend him the money.

AFTER GEORGE

1692

It is likely that death came suddenly to George Fox in August 1691. The 1692 grant of Administration in respect of his goods states that he did not leave a will. The administrator was William Greaves of Woodhouse. The Greaves were neighbours of the Fox family in Bradfield, living in one of the two other substantial houses in the parish, and certainly related by marriage to the Foxes. In his will, the William Fox who died in 1648 left a watch that belonged to his Greaves grandfather (or more likely his great-grandfather). As Administrator William Greaves will have had to enquire into what personal assets George may have owned and the true extent of his debts. There is no record of any Inventory of his personal estate so we do not know if George Fox did indeed die greatly indebted as alleged. What is clear is that More Hall was sold shortly before George's death so the property that passed to his heir was of less value than that which George had inherited. It was, however, still a substantial estate that passed on to his successors.

The Reverend Hunter describes George Fox as having been

"Somewhat festive in character, for it is said that George Fox, along with Bright of Whirlow Hall and Henry Hall at Stumperlowe Hall lived a life of such gaiety or indulgence that, at about the same time, the estates of all three left their possession, wasted away and dissipated. "[45]

Joseph Hunter, a Victorian cleric chooses to blame it all on the Restoration.

"The evil influence of the profligate court of Charles II extended itself through all the graduations of society producing vice, ruin and misery" [46]

Notwithstanding what Hunter had to say on the subject, George Fox passed on Fullwood Hall free of any mortgage. The Smallfield Estate in Bradfield, where his widow and young family were living following his death, together with a share of the Bradfield Rectory tithes and all the family lands around the Hall in Fullwood, including Fullwood Mill and the Hallam fields, all passed on to his heir. All these assets (and others) were retained by the family after his death so it seems somewhat harsh to categorize George as just a dissipated wastrel. To give him credit Hunter did write more positively about George Fox in his work about the minor gentry of Yorkshire. [47] In that book he mentions that "George Fox had the glasshouse at Bolsterstone. " This was essentially a glass-making factory. That asset though did not pass to the son and heir, but was retained and taken to fame and prosperity by George's widow, Mary and at least one of their sons and grandsons.

---

45   Joseph Hunter 1819 Hallamshire pp 206/7
46   Joseph Hunter Hallamshire p 207
47   Joseph Hunter 1895 MS 273 Famille Minorum Gentium p681-4

In 1692 that was still to happen and away from Fullwood Hall, and will be discussed later. The Hall story continues with the new owner, George Fox's eldest surviving son, William Fox, a young man aged 23. As will be seen he was an even more colourful character that his father.

Winter moon rising over Fullwood Hall

CHAPTER 7

THE END OF AN ERA

WILLIAM FOX and his brother GEORGE

1701

On 9th April 1701 the William Fox who had inherited Fullwood Hall less than 10 years previously was buried in Sheffield. His death meant that this was the third consecutive Fox heir who had failed to reach the age of 50. In the Parish records he was not described as a 'Gentleman' like his father, but as a "Yeoman of Fullwood" The reason for this becomes clearer in a case that commenced in December 1701 and was known as Fox v Fox. [48]

The case sets out two versions of the events of the previous decade. When William Fox became the absolute owner of Fullwood Hall in August 1691, his younger brother, George Fox was, we are told, in Flanders. He may have been with the English Army who were occupied there as part of a confederacy fighting Louis XIV of France. George remained in Flanders for around 6 months after his father's death before returning to live at Fullwood Hall which he describes as

"A good Capitale Mansion"

From the time of George's return to the Hall the accounts begin to diverge. On the one side we have Anne Fox a young widow and her two very young children. On the other side is George Fox. Anne is William Fox's widow and George is his brother.

Anne maintains that her husband 'tabled' George at Fullwood Hall. Tabling was the expression used at that time for providing board and lodging. She says he did this for several years and received nothing for it. George says that he was only there for 6-8 months and paid for his accommodation by taking on the management of the estate. He says he then went to live with a Mr Marriott followed by a time with John Ellis (a relative) and then with Samuel Morewood of 'the Oaks' in Bradfield, his mother's old home. He only left the Morewoods when his brother William came to the Oaks and begged him 'tearfully' to return to Fullwood Hall to manage his affairs and to table him there 'as he could not be tabled elsewhere' It seems the farm at Fullwood was let to a Thomas Wilson and Hugh Spooner at this time. The Fox brothers came to an agreement that was formalized by a signed and witnessed agreement dated 5th September 1696. George was to have a lease of the Fullwood estate for 99 years and pay William £30 a year, payable by two instalments, one at the feast of St Michael the Archangel and the other on Lady Day in each year.

---

48   *Fox v Fox National Archives Ref C6/412/76*

George says that the two brothers lived at Fullwood Hall together for two years. Anne says that George abused his position by taking things that were her brothers. George says that the estate was in a poor condition with their grandfather's old corn mill at Fullwood being near collapse and the capital mansion and outbuildings needing re-roofing and repair. He claims he did considerable work in restoring the Hall and the Mill as well as manuring and liming the fields and reclaiming 10 acres from the surrounding moorland, all of which cost him £200.

Creditors were beginning to press William for repayment of his many debts and in December 1697 the brothers mortgaged the Fullwood Estate for £450, according to Anne, and for £400 according to George. It was agreed though that George would have the mortgage money and use it to pay off what were William's very substantial debts. Interest was to be payable at the rate of 6%. While the two brothers were living together in the Hall, George reports that William lived modestly and within his means but eventually William declared that he felt himself 'constrained' and moved out to go and live in Hathersage.

This marks the point where the brothers began their own litigation and accusations and cross-accusations about this period are reported in the 1701 case. Anne accuses George of not paying William's debts and of using the mortgage money to pay his own debts and for his own purposes, She alleges that George kept hunting horses and dogs at Fullwood Hall, costing £100-200 a year, while George accuses his brother of keeping 'a man in livery and horsed' while he was living at Hathersage. Anne says that George abused her husband's 'soft and easy temper' while George describes him as having 'an extravagant temper and much given to excessive drinking'.

In 1698, William's friends intervened to try to get the disputes between the brothers settled. They invited George to attend the house of one of the friends in Tideswell and to bring along an account of what had happened to the mortgage monies he had received as well as the sum of £160 that William received from the sale of three of the Hallom fields (alleged to be the place where Earl Waltheof had his Aula or Hall in the pre-Conquest days.)

William went to Tideswell and, after a few objections by William the accounts were agreed showing a debt by George to William of £60 7s. William however had run up £77 further debt during his 6 months in Hathersage. It was therefore agreed that the £60 7s debt would be forgiven on George taking on the £77 debt and that William would sign over all interest in the Fullwood and Smallfield estates to George in return.

William's friends pointed out that William could not afford to live on £30 a year. He was, after all, the eldest son. It was agreed that the new annual payment would be £35 payable quarterly. All the above was incorporated into written Articles dated 19th October 1698. The conveyances and Deeds of Lease and release were completed on 24th and 25th October in that year. This was the time when the new owner of Fullwood Hall became George Fox. He also owned Smallfield but could not enjoy anything from it until the death of his step-mother who had a life interest there.

By 1699 there had been many changes in the brothers' circumstances. William married Anne Gregory at Ashbourne on 8th November 1698 and George married Anna Broomhead on 3rd June 1699. William's Anne believed that her husband had been hard done by in the previous dealings between the brothers and instigated action. As a result, at the beginning of 1699, William's friends contacted George again. William had run up further debt of £82,12s,11d and they brought him a list of the new debtors. For reasons George does not explain, he sold the remaining Hallom field for £60 and used it to pay off some of the debt despite him losing an income of £3,4s by sale of that asset.

Three new court actions were then brought by William at Anne's instigation (according to George). They allege that George neglected to pay the £35 on the due dates, that he failed to pay the debts when demanded, resulting in William having to go into hiding, being arrested and put in prison and finally that there was an agreement whereby George would reconvey Fullwood Hall to William should William remarry and have children.

George admits that he did not always pay the £35 instalments on the due dates nor did he pay all the debts as demanded but absolutely denies the agreement to reconvey Fullwood Hall to his brother. He does though give some details as to his brother's marriage. He says that Anne was a serving girl working for George at Fullwood Hall where William was being 'tabled' and that she and her friends threatened William with dire consequences if he did not marry her. Their first child was born soon after the marriage and another followed soon after. George points out that she did not bring any dowry.

George says that he was terrified of the probable cost of all the litigation. It is likely that William's friend Henry Balguy, George Fox senior's old nemesis, was acting for William. They were both oldest sons and seem to have been putting pressure on the younger George, so when Thomas Marriott produced an agreement to try, once again, to bring matters to a close, George signed it in the presence of witnesses.

Rather than help, the document created more problems than it solved. The agreement was dated 19th March 1700/1 and had not been prepared by a lawyer, but within three weeks William Fox was dead and buried and it seems that only then did George receive legal advice on the document he had signed and he was horrified at what he heard.

He was told that the agreement stated that the Fullwood Estate would be sold and the proceeds used to pay off the mortgage (upon which it was agreed that nothing had been repaid) and from the surplus £60 of William's old debt and £60 of his new debt would be paid off with any surplus going to George. Until the Smallfield Estate became available on the death of their step-mother, William would receive £10 p.a. during his life and thereafter the sum would be paid to his widow and, on her death, to their children. On the step-mother's death Smallfield would pass to William or whichever of his heirs was alive at the time.

The above was all known to George when he signed the agreement, but his lawyer has pointed out that the £10 p.a. payment would be an incumbrance on the Fullwood estate and would be payable by any purchaser. The children were both very young so potentially payments might have to be made by any purchaser for many years. This would significantly reduce the price anyone would be prepared to pay which would mean that there would be nothing left for George.

George therefore comes up with some extremely weak excuses which were:-

1 He was ill and unable to manage his affairs properly at the time he signed the 1700 agreement.

2 The agreement as written did not absolve George from his obligation to continue to pay the £35 p.a.

3 The agreement was to be replaced by formally drawn up Articles but that could not be done because of Williams early and unexpected death.

These arguments were weak because, ill or not, George signed the agreement in the presence of witnesses. He had no obligation to do so and once signed and witnessed there was no requirement that the agreement should be replaced by Articles and certainly no obligation for any terms to be changed in those Articles. The £35 is irrelevant because William's death brought this obligation to an end without any further payments becoming due.

No doubt under advice (and possibly with gritted teeth) George concludes his answer with an acceptance of an obligation to maintain Anne (his ex-servant) and her children in accordance with his means but asks for the Court not to order specific performance of the agreement as it would mean his bankruptcy and there being no means of servicing the mortgage debt.

There is no record of the outcome of the case but Fullwood Hall certainly remained owned by George Fox until it was sold in 1707 with all the proceeds going to the mortgagee.

What then can we say about the last of the old Fox family to own Fullwood Hall?

The senior George Fox, criticized by Hunter and who died in August 1691, may have run up considerable debts but Fullwood Hall, Smallfield and the Glasshouse all passed on to his successors. When he died there was no mortgage on the Hall and there was still a considerable estate at Fullwood that included several Hallam fields as well as Fullwood Mill, all of which passed on to his eldest son, William.

William seems to have had the idea that he was a gentleman like his father and that a gentleman should not have to deal with mundane matters like earning a living or understanding financial matters. He showed a consistent pattern of carrying on spending money and leaving it to his friends and relations to sort out the details of managing his affairs in general, and the repaying of his many debts in particular. Henry Balgay said of the older George Fox that he was 'very fair at reckoning but very bad at paying' whereas the son William seems to have been unable even to reckon.

The younger brother, George, however is something of an enigma. He is known to have been a Dissenter His Answer in the Court case gives no indication as to how he made his money. The only thing he says in this respect is that he was entitled to his one sixth of the Bradfield tythes (which he sold to help pay his brother's debts).

How then did he obtain the money with which to repay his brother's debts?

We know that he was in Flanders in 1691 but do not know whether he was there on business or engaged either in, or as a supplier to, the army there. Money will have come in from the mill at Fulwood and the fields of the estate were rented out to provide an income. It is said that the payment of £35 p.a. to William was agreed because this was the rent that was being paid by the farm tenants in 1698. George's answer goes into meticulous detail as to the amount of the 1698 and later debt that he had cleared or promised to pay. He must therefore have been receiving enough to pay these and maintain himself and his own family following his own marriage to Anna Broomhead in 1699. He probably maintained his brother's widow and children after the Court case, but this is unlikely to have cost more than the £35 p.a. he was paying to his brother. Why then does it seem that nothing was ever repaid on the Fullwood Hall mortgage and the whole of the sale proceeds went to the mortgagee when Fullwood Hall was sold in 1707?

Perhaps George will never have expected to have Fullwood Hall whilst growing up, so it may be that keeping it was never a priority of his and that he was better at robbing Peter to pay Paul than his older brother so he was adept at juggling his personal income and outgoings. By the end of 1707 the mortgage debt will have risen to well over £700 assuming compound interest added annually at 6% and no payments being made. No doubt the mortgagee will also have had costs in calling in the debt and the costs of sale will also have to have been paid. The purchaser of the estate had already obtained assignment of a judgment of a debt that George Fox, the owner of the Hall, had to the Sitwell family. As a result, it is no surprise that the whole of the 1707 sale proceeds went to the mortgagee.

George and Anna had their son, also called George, christened at the Upper Chapel in Sheffield in 1702. George was a Trustee there. Another son, John, was reported by Hunter as working as a young framework knitter (whilst still a minor) in the Midlands in 1717, so he was likely to have been living at the Hall up to the time of sale. His father, the last Fox occupant of the Hall is probably the 'George Fox Gent' who is reported to have been buried in Sheffield on 29th July 1718. The last owner was dead and the old Fox dynasty at Fullwood Hall came to an end. It had lasted for nearly three hundred years.

The Fox family however did not entirely disappear from the Mayfield Valley following the loss of the Hall. The William Fox who died in 1580 left 8 sons, and one or more of these helped ensure that the name would continue in the region for centuries to come. Not though as gentlemen. These Foxes were all farmers. Their details are contained in an appendix for anyone wishing to claim descent.

Sunrise

CHAPTER 8

YET MORE FOXES

George's Second Family

As described, 1707 marked the end of the Fox family ownership of Fullwood Hall. Somewhat confusingly the new owner is also called Fox, but he is not related to the previous occupiers and it is not yet time for his story.

Before following what happened to the Hall's new inheritor, the story of George Fox's widow, Mary, and their five children, follows, but, before that, here is a short table introducing them with their years of birth. George's first family have already been described and now it is the second family's turn.

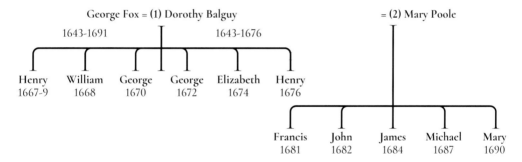

Table 2 Children of George Fox and his two wives

George Fox's widow, Mary Fox, (nee Pole) remarried a George Blackburn in 1702. Her story is a fascinating one as she seems to have made a fortune for herself and her successors from her connection with her first husband, George Fox's glassworks at Bolsterstone. The reason she retained it rather than it passing directly to George's oldest son by his first marriage is likely to be because George Fox only had a life interest in the Glass works. This may be due to his marriage settlement with Mary. It is likely that any investment by the very wealthy Pole family in the union between George and Mary would have been protected by the device known as 'Jointure' whereby it was the husbands to use during his life but would pass for the benefit of the wife, if she survived him for the rest of her life and then would pass to the children of George and Mary as provided in the deed. This certainly was the case with George's first marriage and it is more than likely that jointure explains the survival of that asset with Mary nominating which of her children would have it after her death. [49] What is known of those children is as follows :-

The eldest, Francis, was said to be a 'painter' by Hunter but was probably what

---

[49] *Mary Fox's will is held by the Borthwick institute Registered Probate ref Vol 87 folio 99 MF 1006*

we would call a religious artist. He was certainly still alive in 1738 as he was a substantial beneficiary named in his mother's will of that date.

James (Jacobus in the Parish Register) is reported by Hunter as having been baptized by a Jesuit priest (although there is no record of this in the parish register at Bradfield.) It is almost certain that he re-appears in the area as a Catholic priest as the 'missioner' for Bolsterstone and Bradfield chapels under the name of James Pole (or Poole alias ffoxe S J) 'until 1739 or later'. [50] As taking Mass for a priest was still, technically, punishable by death at this time, (although not enforced) it was normal for priests who had been trained on the Continent to assume a name other than their own. The S J shows that he was a Jesuit. He died, in Derbyshire, in 1760. [51]

Little is known of Michael and it is possible that he too was a priest. Hunter reports that on Michael's death he left a rather special watch made by Randulph Bull who was watchmaker to Queen Elizabeth from 1587. It belonged to his mother Mary Fox so will have spent some of its life at Fullwood Hall. It is described as

The face engraven. Double gilt. The works nearly an inch deep, with the case stands an inch and a half high. Heavy. Has a handle with a ring to hang by the side or to put into the pockets. Engraven upon it seems to be

A chevron between three cranes necks

Three cups

3 foxes heads and fess dansette (/\/\/\ )

A chevron between three escallops & border engrailed with Baronet's mark

Crest a cranes head out of a coronet

Motto 'Pavis negatur gloria magna quies'[52] (Striking negates the glory of great peace)

It is intriguing to see the reference to the foxes' heads and it is possible that it was a gift to Mary from her husband George Fox. It calls to mind George's fondness for gambling. Could he have won it in a card game or bought it because of the fox engraving, or even some connection with the family of John Fox (the 1707 purchaser of the Hall) who had the three foxes head on his coat of Arms? Hunter's description enables the watch to be dated between 1611, when Baronets were first created and 1617 when Randolph Bull died.

John Fox and his son Michael were both heavily involved with the glassworks.

A local antiquary, John Wilson (1719-1783) of Broomhead Hall, wrote about the glassworks in 1779

"(In Bate Green) *there is a glasshouse for making glass which was erected by... (Fox), a Roman Catholic and enjoyed by his widow after his death for many years. Brought to great perfection by Mr Blackburn and Mr William Finney his manager*"[53]

William Finney, the manager of the glass house married the youngest of Mary's

50   *Archbishop Herrings Visitation Returns 1743 vol iv pp 73 &75*

51   *Ibid contained in Appendix A notes*

52   *Joseph Hunter 1895 MS 273 Famille Minorum Gentium p681-4*

53   *As reported in Joseph Kenworthy Handbook No 6 to The Early History of Stocksbridge & District Bolsterstone Glass House and its place in the History of English Glass Making*

children, her only daughter, who was also called Mary

Kenworthy writes that the small glassmaking business being carried out by the earlier John Fox from Smallfield, was later moved to the glass house 'had' by George Fox, at Bate Green in what is now Stocksbridge.

On the outstanding quality of the products, Wilson writes

"The glass made here is so famed that it is carried to London and other places and there sold at higher prices than London glass. "

In support of this, there is a story, again reported by Wilson, that the female occupants of Underbank Hall demanded a full set of fine glassware and that their lawyer father, a Mr Fenton, promised to acquire the same on his next trip to London. On being shown a particularly fine set, in London, he asked where the glass had come from. When he was told it was 'Bolsterstone Glass' he was amazed as he had no knowledge that the glasses that he was looking at could have been purchased, by him, barely a mile away from his own home![54]

The drinking glasses made are certainly stylish and elegant. Examples can be seen displayed at a small museum in the Town Hall at Stocksbridge. They owe their existence to George and Mary Fox of Fullwood Hall, their son John and his son Michael. This is acknowledged in a poster at the museum which shows a selection of the glasshouse wares. Presumably George and Mary drank their wine at Fullwood Hall from glasses made at their Glassworks at Bolsterstone

In the course of writing this book, Yvonne Summerfield, one of the Fox family descendants, sent us a photograph of a large Bolsterstone glass that has been passed down to her through the generations. She has kindly given permission for us to reproduce it here. At 6 ½ inches tall and with a generous bowl and short stem it is what is known as a 'Rummer'. Other glasses from the museum are also shown.

---

54   *Joseph Kenworthy Handbook No 6 to The Early History of Stocksbridge & District Bolsterstone Glass House and its place in the History of English Glass Making' p15*

Photo.   **No. 5.**   J. Bradbury.

Thirteen representative specimens of Drinking-glasses made at the Bolsterstone Glass House.
A.D. 1670-1740.

The heirloom 'rummer' glass and some museum glasses

A similar, but decorated glass is also shown being admired by Roger Hostombe at the Stocksbridge Museum

Spring 2023 Roger Hostombe at Stocksbridge museum with a Bolsterstone glass

So, we come to the end of an era. The Fox family married into the Fullwood Estate of the Lynotts in the 1420's and were responsible for the conversion of the old medieval house to a half-timbered Hall, extending the house in the later Tudor period and, by 1620, the appearance of the Hall would have been much as it is today. No less than 10 generations were involved before their connection with Fullwood Hall was terminated by the sale in 1707. It is only fitting that their names and dates are recorded here.

Name		Birth	Married to	Death	Notes
John Lynott	1391				Messuage to self and heirs
Adam Lynott			Isola	1428	Inherits from John
Agnes Lynott	1428		John Fox	1458	Inherits from her father. Husband John Fox acquires land in Okenhale in 1439
Thomas Fox	1458			1490	Inherits on death of his mother, Agnes.
Thomas Fox	1490			1515/6	Inherits from his father Acquires Okenholt land 1509
Robert Fox	1515/6	c 1490	Emmot	1544	Inherits from his father
William Fox	1543	c 1522	(1) Dionysia? 1563 (2) Margaret	1580	Acquires from his father shortly before his Father's death
William Fox	1580	c 1545	(1) Jennetta ? (2) Joanne	1612	His father's successor
Ulysses Fox	1612	1575/6 (R)	Elizabeth Greene 1612	April 1649	His Father's successor. Extends Hall 1620
William Fox	Dies before his father Ulysses	1613	Anne Morewood 1636	Oct 1648	Does not inherit
George Fox	1649	1642/3	(1) Dorothy Balguy 1665 (2) Mary Pole 1679	Aug 1691	Not able to take until he is 21
William Fox	1691	1668	Anne Gregory 1698	1701	Inherits on his father's death
George Fox	1698	1670	Dorothy Broomhead 1699	Post 1707	Acquires brother's interest but sells in 1707

Table 3 The Lynotts and ten generations of the Foxes

The Fullwood Hall story now turns to the next occupant whose purchase was completed in 1707. His name was John Fox. His family were not related to the previous Fox occupants, and the Catholicism of Mary Fox and her children was to be replaced by a new attitude to religion as will be seen very shortly.

CHAPTER 9

A DIFFERENT KIND OF FOX

JOHN FOX

1714

If, indeed, George Fox had been a Catholic sympathising bon-viveur and entrepreneur, it would be hard to think of a greater contrast between two men than that between him and the new owner of Fullwood Hall, John Fox, who bought the Hall in 1707 and whose family descended from charcoal burners on the site of the old Beauchief Abbey approximately 20 years after its dissolution. He has a house in Dixon Lane Sheffield, and is certainly a wealthy man.

He is unmarried and without children, He is a godly and public-spirited man but not a supporter of either the Catholic faith or the establishment Church of England. He is what is known as a Dissenter.

He had purchased Fullwood Hall seven years previously after buying up some of the old Fox property that had been sold to go towards their ever-mounting debts. He had also obtained a judgment against the owner of the Hall, so was in a strong position to force a sale. He is now settled at Fullwood Hall and is aware of the lack of religious provision for the growing community of Dissenters in and around Fulwood. In those days 'the 5 Mile Act' made it an offence for clergymen to reside anywhere within 5 miles of a parish from which they had been expelled for refusing to conform to the established church practices. Such clergy and many of their old flock of worshippers formed the group that had become known by the name of 'Dissenters.'

Fulwood and the surrounding area have many individuals who hold similar religious views to John Fox. They are holding their services in the very remote 'Lord's Seat' way out on the moors. These are likely to have included John Fox's friend, William Ronksley, who would later help found the small chapel that is still non-denominational and operating in Fulwood.

Lord's Seat was more than 5 miles away from Sheffield. It was a long and arduous journey over the stony and muddy tracks and extremely difficult in bad weather.

John Fox has just found a way to make things a little easier. As the roads were much less direct in those days, Sheffield Parish Church was also more than 5 miles from Fullwood Hall so it would be legal to have preaching there. Religious services could be held indoors if the place was first licensed. John Fox has already applied for such a license for an upstairs room at Fullwood Hall and is overjoyed that his application has been granted.

Where though was this 'upstairs room'? It would be normal to assume that the worship took place in the Hall itself, but the present garage has a set of substantial steps leading up to what is now the roof. In John Fox's day though there was an upper storey, so, it may well be that this is where the worship took place. This may explain the cross-shaped window in the downstairs of that building which would be converted to a use as a garage by Morgan Fairest in the 20th century. There are certainly several examples of worship being conducted in the upstairs storey of buildings in and around the Mayfield Valley later and none of the upstairs rooms at the Hall itself are promising candidates for being the site where a congregation of any number could meet.

There is a building shown on the plans for Fullwood Hall, prepared in 1781, in the position of the current garage, that building would have had a direct frontage to Fulwood Common so would be easy to access. It may well be that this building is indeed where the worship took place and the cross shaped window and the remnants of arches incorporated into the ground floor and the inside of the building, may be there as re-use of stone or in commemoration of the building's history as a place where worship once took place.

'Religious' windows in the garage

Steps to the old preaching house

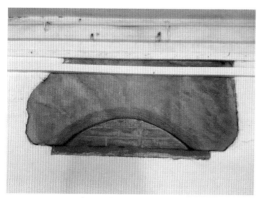

Arch inside garage – A niche?

Arch behind garage

Were the arches shown above part of a different building near to the Hall back then? Did they form part of the 1714 Dissenters' licensed building? Or do they hark back to an even older use of this part of the building for religious purposes? Who knows? A brief geo-physical investigation has revealed anomalies below the level of the present floor, so there are certainly plenty of questions. Whatever the answers this building certainly has a long-standing connection to the Hall and the Dissenting community of Fulwood and the West of Sheffield will have certainly been very grateful to have had the use of it!

"Hall Meadow and Stubbing" paintings by Caroline Holley

John Fox has died a wealthy man. He has left a considerable amount of money and property to good causes, both in his lifetime and in his will. He not only owned Fullwood Hall (as copyhold from the Duke of Norfolk) and the freehold of the Bank, Broad and Daw fields adjoining the Hall, but also other houses and land in Fulwood, an estate in Wadsley, another at Owlerton, (both now suburbs of Sheffield) and yet another in Norton Lees (then in Derbyshire), he also owned a dwellinghouse in Church Lane Sheffield. Like George Fox he adopted a coat of Arms. His though, was a chevron with 3 foxes' heads as opposed to George's bear with an axe. It is possible that he was the John Fox, Gentleman, who held the responsible and prestigious position of the Collector of Rents for the Town Burgesses in 1707 and 1708. If it was him the Town Trustees very much approved of him as acting collector following the death of the previous collector as, at the end of his year of office, they entered a memorandum in their records that all future collectors should give notice of at least 3 days via the Bellman of the date on which they were due to present their accounts,[55] a practice first adopted by John Fox.

His gift to the school in Fulwood was the considerable sum of £150 '*for the maintenance of a schoolmaster to teach the children to read and write*', he benefitted the Hollis Hospital in Sheffield (including giving forty shillings to be divided between the inhabitants at the following Christmas) and provided a sum to ensure the Upper Meeting House in Sheffield could have a minister to conduct their services.

The generosity of John Fox is commemorated by a plaque placed high up on the school that he helped to fund. The school was attended by local children for more than 150 years until the local education board decided to have a new School constructed at the bottom of David Lane in the late 1870's.

The old school is now a private house, but the plaque remains.

---

55   *The Record of the Burgers of Sheffield by J D Leader (1897) p325*

Plaque in old school wall

Although he leaves no children himself, John Fox does have relatives. His sister Mary has three daughters and a son who had died before John Fox made his will. One of the daughters, Dorothy Oliver, is living at Fullwood Hall with her gentleman husband James. They are paying £50 a year rent. Dorothy is certainly John's favourite niece as he has left her a life interest in the Hall and, on her death, it should pass to her eldest son, or eldest daughter, if there were no sons.

Dorothy and James already have a baby daughter, Sarah born at Fullwood Hall in the year before John's death so John must have felt that the future of Fullwood Hall was settled. Dorothy is aged 39 but possibly pregnant again. Given the uncertainties of life at this time John has made provision as to what should happen if Dorothy's line were to fail.

What happened will be discovered in the next chapter.

CHAPTER 10

MORE TRUSTEES

1746

Dorothy Oliver has continued to live at Fullwood Hall. Her first husband has died and she has remarried a clergyman, George Hampton. Accordingly her name is now, or more accurately was, 'Hampton', as this is the name that now describes her in her burial record. She has just died aged 58. John Fox had hoped that she might have had a son or daughter to succeed her, but that was not to be. Her daughter Sarah died in 1740 aged 20 and unmarried, and another daughter born shortly after John's death did not survive infancy. Lawyers have had to be consulted to decide what is to happen next.

John Fox's old 1721 will has been found and the provisions poured over to discover what was to happen to Fullwood Hall. Fortunately, John Fox had clearly stated what he wanted to happen in these circumstances. Less fortunately it meant that there was to be no single person to benefit and that no less than six people have an equal one sixth share in the Hall. As a result, none of them can live in the Hall without the others agreement.

The beneficiaries are all female. They are John Fox's only surviving niece, Elizabeth Shemeld, Hannah, the daughter of his deceased niece, Mary Gervas, now married and known as Hannah Hawke, and the 4 daughters of John's deceased niece, Mary Gervas, namely Elizabeth, Anne, Sarah, and Rebecca.

1752

John Fox's original Trustees had been men that he trusted and were of his own faith. None of those were still alive in 1746 when his niece Dorothy died and so the Trustees appointed to look after the six female beneficiaries were their respective husbands. Hannah Hawke and her husband had, very quickly recorded Hannah's one sixth interest in Fullwood Hall and it appears in the Court Rolls for the manor of Sheffield of 1746

At this point, however, it may be helpful to explain, in simplified form, the different types of land ownership that existed in this period. At its simplest, you could hold land in one of three ways.

All land technically belonged to the Crown but, for all those not the monarch, the highest form of ownership was the freehold. Historically this was held by the Lord of the Manor. Those holding land directly from him were called copyholders. The reason for the name was that their ownership was recorded in the local Court Rolls. A sale was made by the old copyholder agreeing to surrender his rights back to the Lord of the Manor and the Lord agreeing to accept the new copyholder on payment of what was called a 'fine.' The fine was a set amount of money based on the value of the land being transferred. The amount had been fixed in the very distant past. Both the surrender by the old occupier and the acceptance of the new copyholder were recorded in the Rolls after the transaction was explained at one of the Lords regular courts set up for that purpose

The copyholder did not need to personally occupy the land. He was free to agree to allow occupation to a tenant who would pay him, or her, rent. Tenants were the third group of land holders. They too might rent out a field or two to their own sub-tenants.

In 1746, the Trustees and the beneficiaries were all related, but, by 1752, some have already sold their interests to outsiders (like Samuel Shore, a well-known local banker) so the trust is no longer just a family matter. An offer has been made to purchase Fullwood Hall and the offer has been considered by the Trustees and the beneficiaries. They have been informed that the intended purchaser is a reliable and wealthy cleric from the Barnsley area and that the price offered is a good one. They have just decided to accept the offer.

The new intended owner's name is John Clarkson and he is to be introduced in the next chapter.

CHAPTER 11

THE CLARKSON FAMILY

THE REVEREND JOHN CLARKSON

1757

John Clarkson is not a well man, He is the vicar of Silkstone near Barnsley and a man wealthy enough to have set up a school in Silkstone with an endowment of a house, a cottage and 5 acres of land shortly after buying Fullwood Hall. He re-assures his 5 daughters that they will all be provided for as his will made four years previously gives them each a one-fifth interest in his premises subject only to payment of an annuity of £35 a year to their brother John. Only one of his daughters is unmarried and her one-fifth share will keep her comfortably and not exactly harm her marriage prospects. In keeping with this somewhat 'Pride and Prejudice' theme, one of his trustees is a son-in-law called Mr Bingley.

John is living near his church in Silkstone and not in Fullwood Hall which is tenanted so the rent will be used towards the daughters' maintenance.

The Conveyance to him in 1752 contained the rights for him to use the pews in the Parish Church of Sheffield or in the chapels at Bradfield and Ecclesall all of which belonged to Fullwood Hall. This would have been something of a 'busman's holiday' for the Rev Clarkson' if he ever used the right!

1780

John Clarkson did not survive to the end of 1757. There has been a trust for 23 years benefitting John Clarkson's 5 daughters and their issue.

In 1780, the legal position at Fullwood Hall is that The Earl of Surrey owns the freehold of the Hall and much of the land. That Earlship is a subsidiary title of a much more familiar one, the Duke of Norfolk, who, as Lord of the Manor, owns most of the land in and around Fulwood. The copyhold is held by many Trustees who have already borrowed £500 from George Greaves, a successful merchant in Sheffield. As security they are giving him a mortgage of Fullwood Hall. George Hallam is stated to be the tenant and a long list of gentlemen are stated to be the legal owners. They are:-

William Green of Berners Street London, Luck Arnnigan of Kirby, William Walker, surgeon and apothecary of Penistone, Thomas Sutcliffe of Dodworth Green, Jonathan West (the younger) of Barnsley and John Knight (the younger) of London.[56]

The illustrious sounding group are the current Trustees under the will of John Clarkson. All, except William Green, were entitled through their wives who were daughters of John Clarkson or through their children. William Green was the son of one of the daughters. Why they have borrowed money from George Greaves is known to them but not to us. We do though learn something of Fullwood Hall from the Deed though as, for the first time, the names of the fields that were part of the then 36 acres Estate were listed. These were

'Long Oakney, Great Oakney, 3 Nooked Oakney, Calf Croft, Hall Field, The Stubbins, Hall Meadow, Ing Meadow, Well Field, and the Water Stubbin.

Fullwood Hall is a working farm in 1780 and has been for some considerable time. John Fox's niece Dorothy died in 1746 and since then the Hall has been owned either by trustees for various daughters or by an investor. It is almost certain that no money has been spent on anything more than the sort of temporary repairs that you might expect of a tenant. The condition of the property may well explain what happened next in the Hall's history.

---

56   *Bagshawe Muniments (13/10/181)*

CHAPTER 12

A NEW ORDER – THE GREAVES

1784/5

The Clarkson interest has come to an end. By 1784 their Trustees debt to the affluent Sheffield merchant George Greaves has risen to £1,000 and they have sold Fullwood Hall 'now or lately in the occupation of William Fox' to George Greaves. Accordingly, the Greaves family have now acquired the copyhold interest in the Hall.

The tenant, William Fox had been living with his family at the Hall, but he has died and George Greaves has opened negotiations with the Land Agent for the Duke of Norfolk for the acquisition of the freehold. If successful this will be the first time in the Hall's history that the copyhold and the freehold will be in the same hands.

In 1785 a price is agreed after negotiation. It is fixed in the sum of £33, and the Conveyance is made by the Duke, acting in his subsidiary title, the Earl of Surrey. The Hall, and all the fields mentioned in the 1780 mortgage will therefore shortly have a new absolute owner who has the financial resources and the desire to do something about the state of the buildings.

Fullwood Hall was certainly not intended as a home for the Greaves family as George Greaves had already bought Page Hall in Sheffield, described as the first great house built on the fruits of the great wealth coming in to Sheffield from its growing industries. When it was being constructed, locals are reputed to have muttered, darkly, that no good would come of such extravagance. They were proved right as the original owner of Page Hall ran out of money before he had finished the building and had to sell it before the planned work was finished. Soon after it was purchased by George Greaves. George Bustard Greaves, his only son, would marry a wealthy heiress Ellen Cley in December 1785 and George would give his son Page Hall as a home for the new family. He has already ensured that his son would have Fullwood Hall and the younger George has rapidly found a tenant with whom he can work to achieve mutual benefit. The freehold of Fullwood Hall was conveyed to him in 1785.

On 30th December 1784 there is an agreement by the new tenant of Fullwood Hall, Robert Marshall, to pay interest on the money spent by George Bustard Greaves in improving the land allocated to the tenant of the farm by earlier enclosure.

Enclosure may well have been the reason the Greaves were interested in Fullwood Hall. The Hall lands were surrounded by local Commons and Village Greens that were essentially common property used by local inhabitants. There had already been enclosure in Hallam which had benefited the Hall and it will have been known that further enclosure was planned and which would give the Estate further land to enable the improvement in agricultural practice (according to the stated reasons for enclosure). It was also a way of ensuring that landowners could obtain land and more convenient roads at the expense of those previously exercising rights over the communal Commons and Greens.

Whatever the rights and wrongs of enclosure, the relationship between the Greaves and the Marshall families will last for over a hundred years. First though, it is time to introduce one of the more interesting characters in Sheffield history.

GEORGE BUSTARD GREAVES

The new owner of Fullwood Hall, George Bustard Greaves, would not be out of place in a Charles Dickens novel.

He was an impressive character, and to demonstrate his flamboyant style, he would ride around in a yellow carriage (itself a novelty in those days). His liverymen wore bright light-blue breeches. He, however, in his later life, favoured wearing an old-fashioned wig (a bag-wig) and dressing in a blue coat with metal buttons and buckskin breeches. In a speech recalling him, made in 1878, Sheffield's Alderman Moore is reported as describing him as a portly man who

"Kept a stable full of horses, a house full of young men, and a cellar full of good wine. Many a happy hour he spent at Page Hall in those days and young people never left it without the master putting a half-crown into the boy's hand. "

Moving swiftly on, George Bustard Greaves had his portrait painted by a well-known and fashionable artist, George Romney, the sitter seated in aristocratic pose. A much inferior painting by one of the authors of this book shows an approximation of his appearance.

George Bustard Greaves (or something like!)

George Bustard Greaves would die an exceedingly wealthy man in 1835. He was father to four sons and rich enough to leave each of his sons a substantial house and estate on his death. His youngest son, Henry Marwood Greaves, of Matlock, would inherit Fullwood Hall. Five years before his death George Bustard Greaves would also buy the well-known Strines Inn, just over the Derbyshire border, to add to his already considerable property portfolio.

George would invest heavily in Fullwood Hall, As well as the 1784 agreement with Robert Marshall, and the grant of a 15-year lease to Robert in 1788, there is, in the Rylands library in Manchester a folder that contains many bills detailing the work that was being carried out at the Hall in the period 1784 - 1796. [57]

Having given a brief description and portrayal of the man who owned Fullwood Hall, we now need to return to the Hall itself. At the same time as we first see painted representations of one of the owners, we also begin to have plans which show the Hall and its land and the above-mentioned evidence which shows the extensive work that was being carried out around the Hall for the benefit of George Bustard Greaves and his tenant, Robert Marshall.

57 *Bagshawe Muniments ref 13/10/188*

CHAPTER 13

CHANGES 1781 to 1854

As indicated, it is time to move away for a while from the owners and occupiers. The 1793 Sheffield Enclosure Act involved a survey of all land in the Fulwood area with a view to the creation of new roads and the apportionment of Common Land between owners and those enjoying certain rights over the land. Documents produced in this period, and before, by the Fairbanks firm of Surveyors give us plans and the name of fields as well as the names of the owners. From this time onwards we begin to have more specific information about Fullwood Hall and the land held and managed by its owners and tenants.

The owner, George Bustard Greaves, was awarded considerable Common Land under the Sheffield Enclosure Act of 1793 and the Fullwood Hall tenant, Robert Marshall, also benefitted from that Act and the earlier enclosures already described.

Reproduced here is part of a plan prepared by the firm of Fairbanks for the John Clarkson Trustees in 1781. This is the first reliable map showing the building [58]

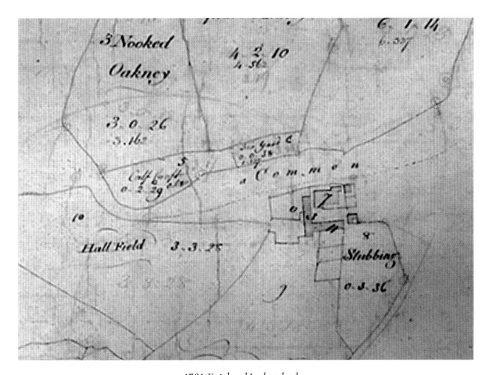

1781 Fairbank's sketch plan

58   *Plan extract reproduced by courtesy of Sheffield City Archives, Fairbanks Collection, Ref. FC/MB/402 S*

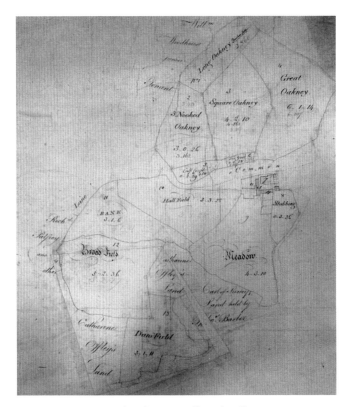

Larger plan showing Fullwood Hall 1781

The next plan shows the Hall itself, a small yard adjacent to field 137 and a few buildings open to the road. It is not to scale[59]

Enlarged plan showing Fullwood Hall in 1791

59 *Reproduced by courtesy of Sheffield City Archives, Fairbanks Collection, Ref. FC/P/She/118 S*

The first thing that is immediately noticeable is that the Hall itself opens directly onto what was to become Harrison Lane and David Lane. The building shown on the other side of the road is the property now known as 'The Hole in the Wall' but previously 'David Lane Farm' and, before that, 'Hall Farm.'

By 1824, a Tithe plan[60] shows a different configuration. The road is now defined and walls have begun to appear to enclose part of the Fullwood Hall Land.

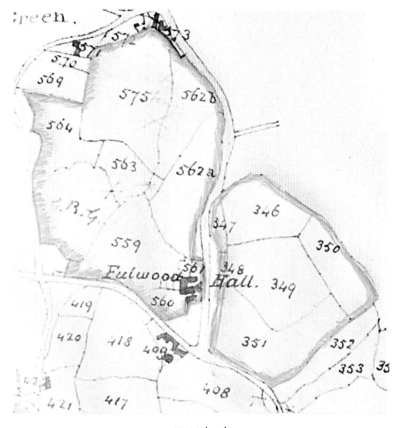

1824 Tithe plan

The fields will be described in the next chapter. The green edging on the plan indicates the majority of the Fullwood Hall estate in 1824 (but not the parts enclosed in the 1790's.) The initials 'GBG' on one of the fields indicates that this field also belonged to George Bustard Greaves as did the areas granted to the Hall by the Inclosure Act.

By the time of the 1854 1st edition of the Ordnance Survey Map the present front entrance to the Hall has been completed and a drive and access has been formed onto Harrison Lane. Prior to that it would have been quite a substantial house that you would have seen facing you as you approached up the hill but not the main facade.

As well as the changes to Fullwood Hall it is interesting to note how the intersection of Harrison Lane with David Lane (at that time called 'Hall Lane') has migrated

60   *Reproduced by courtesy of Sheffield City Archives, Fairbanks Collection, Ref. FC/MB/484*

much further away from both Fullwood Hall and 'The Hole in the Wall' (then called 'Hall Farm') This may well have had something to do with the occupier of Fullwood Hall, John Marshall, being an Overseer in Upper Hallam and having responsibility for the roads in Fulwood in the 1830's and 1840's. If you visit the area, you will be struck by the difference in height between the two-house sites. The present road down David Lane is steep enough. The pre 1854 road may well have been even steeper!

1854 OS plan showing fully enclosed site

The additional land, mentioned above, that had accrued to the Hall had come from the enclosure of Fullwood Hall Common as can be seen from the following plan where the darker colouring around the Hall along what is now Harrison Lane and South and East of the Hall shows the land acquired. Apart from Harrison Lane itself it will be seen that all the old Fullwood Hall Common was allocated to the Hall owner.

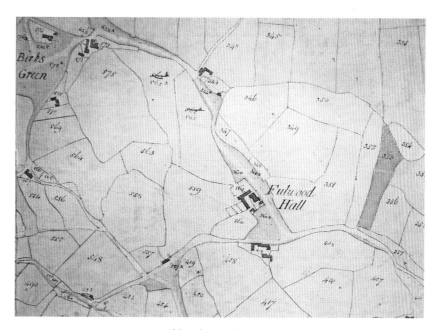

Old enclosures 1792 plan

The plan is a small part of a much larger plan that shows how all the old Commons were allocated. [61] Harrison Lane can be seen running through the land by the Hall, The more northerly triangular piece of land was allocated to Bole Hill Farm. In those days Fullwood Hall had few other neighbours. What is now Bennet Grange, Bennet Grange Cottages, Bents Green Farm and Jeffrey Green Cottages, all to the north-west, Mill Lane Farm is to the West, the row of cottages to the south-west and the Hole-in-the-Wall farm to the South were the only occupied sites in this part of Fulwood. As already mentioned, When the Greaves family acquired the Hall freehold in 1784/5, they set about a considerable programme of repair and renovation. In addition to the re-roofing a vast number of ground clearers and levellers, stone pit fillers (in Calf Croft), a pump maker, carpenters, wall builders, gate makers, lead workers, and general labourers were to send bills to the owners. Part of some of the early bills was paid by William Fox, the pre-1785 tenant. It is likely that these were for dilapidations arising during his tenancy and which would have been his responsibility. There was also the agreement by Robert Marshall to be responsible for interest on payments for certain clearance works on land that had been allocated to the Hall tenant.

The buildings described in the roofing bill for the Hall comprised:-

The Hall itself, a large slate-roofed barn and stables, a cowhouse, a gateway, a pigsty, a kitchen, and a separate slop kitchen. All were re-roofed. The small building to the right of the Hall and at right angles to Harrison Lane shown on the previous plan, may well have been one of these buildings. When the wall between the road and the Hall was built the end wall of that building was incorporated into the wall, leaving two blocked-up upstairs windows that are still there. The rest of the building will have disappeared long ago!

---

61 *Plan extract reproduced by courtesy of Sheffield City Archives, Fairbanks Collection, Ref. FC/P/She/128 L*

One of the upstairs blocked-up windows on Harrison Lane

It is at this time that the stone footpath was constructed down 'Hall Hill' and a new pump installed. At the bottom of the hill, next to the path, we discovered a rectangular underground chamber with pipes entering and leaving it under a very large stone. This structure was found as part of our 'tunnel' investigations described in the last chapter of this book. The reservoir is likely to have stored the water for the pump, but it is hard to work out why a pump should be put so far away from the Hall. The fields are all adequately supplied with water. Indeed, one is known as 'the Carr', which means a wet or marshy place. The Hall itself was supplied by a stream running right past it as evidenced by the collection of water troughs sited along the water course that passed right next to the Hall.

Like the reasons for the reservoir, or whatever it may be, being constructed where it was, we know little about other outbuildings at the time, apart from the description of the buildings that were re-roofed and the fact that Fullwood Hall was stated to have 7 hearths in 1672 in the Hearth Tax returns for Lady Day in that year. Below is reproduced the roofing bill from John Froggatt dated 1785. [62]

62   *Reproduced by courtesy of The John Rylands Research Institute & Library copyright of The University of Manchester.*

Roofing bill for the Hall 1785

In addition to the above, one of Robert Marshall's relatives, Joseph Marshall, built 14 'roods' of causeway (a rood is probably 5½ yards at this time) and spent 5 days labouring to level the ground for a new wall before building a wall claimed to be 54 roods. This is likely to be the wall separating the Hall from Harrison Lane. It was built in 1794/5. There was also money spent on 'ridding' the land acquired under the enclosure acts of stone and other impediments to agricultural uses. In addition to Common land around the Hall, George Bustard Greaves was awarded over 89 acres of moorland under the Act but exchanged it for several fields and woodland belonging to the Duke of Norfolk, to the West of the Hall land.

Although the cost of the various work was considerable, George could certainly afford it. His Fullwood Hall Estate was substantial.

In 1824 George paid the sum of £2 by way of tithe in respect of just over 50 acres of land he owned in Fulwood. Only Catherine Offley, with 78 acres, and William Murray, with 51 acres, owned more land in Upper Hallam. An article written in 1887 confirmed that the owner of Fullwood Hall at that time was Henry Marwood Greaves. [63] In 1897, however, the Estate was sold, thus ending the Greaves' long period of ownership of Fullwood Hall.

Muriel Hall, in her excellent book 'The Mayfield Valley' explains how 'The Hole in the Wall' received its name and a connection with Fullwood Hall.

---

63   *Sheffield Weekly Telegraph 12th November 1887 (which also has an inaccurate drawing of the Hall!)*

The book explains that Fullwood Hall itself received the benefit of an excellent spring that supplied water to the Hall and farm. There are still several troughs on site that used to receive water directly from this spring. After leaving Fullwood Hall the spring continued directly down the hill to The Hole in the Wall Farm. When the area was open this was not a problem. As can be seen from the plans, walls were erected in the 19th century and to continue the water supply a hole was left in the wall on the Fullwood Hall side of David Lane. The spring then was channelled under the road to the farm on the other side of the Lane. It seems that an ornamental arch was built over the position where the spring came through the wall.

As is the nature of springs, this one seems to have changed its course and ceased to flow through the arch. Those at the farm dug a new well and the arch continued to stand with only a hill bank behind it. During the years when the Rivelin reservoirs were being constructed, workmen were supplied with ale at several local farms. 'The Hole in the Wall' is said to have been the name given by the navvies to this ale house, as, to them, it was opposite an arch to nowhere. A later owner of Fullwood Hall, Frederick Oates is said to have removed the arch to re-use the stone elsewhere. When he had finished the removal of the arch, he is reputed to have said to Mrs Fox who lived on the other side of the lane.

"I'll leave thee t'hole in t'wall" [64]

Old stone troughs at the Hall

---

64 Muriel Hall 'The Mayfield Valley' p22

CHAPTER 14

THE MARSHALL FAMILY AND EVENTS

1784 to 1867

The Marshall family have already been introduced. The first of them to live at Fullwood Hall, was Robert Marshall, who was tenant in late 1784, and, in 1788, was granted a lease of the Hall for fifteen years from George Bustard Greaves. Little is known of Robert other than that he came from Stannington and is likely to be the Robert Marshall the son of John Marshall of Storrs, who was baptized at Bradfield on 30th Dec 1759.

It seems that Robert Marshall was married to Gertrude Hawke because in her obituary in 1841 (she had died in Sheffield, aged eighty-six) she was described as 'the widow of the late Robert Marshall of Fullwood Hall'. When he married Gertrude at Bradfield on 6th March 1806, Robert already had a son named John who had been born in 1797, possibly in Fullwood Hall. He farmed over fifty acres which was a very substantial amount for that period. The fields he farmed in 1795 are shown in the following table:-

Field No	Field Name	Field No	Field Name
346	3 Nooked Oakney	554	Wood Close
347	Calf Croft	559	Meadow
348	Fir Yard	560	Stubbing
349	Square Oakney	561	Fullwood Hall
350	Long Oakney	562a	Hall Field
351	Great Oakney	562b	Bank Field
485	Ing Meadow	563	Nether Meadow
494	Well Field	564	Daw Field
551	Water Stubbing	575	Broad Field

Table 4 Field Names

When Robert purchased some additional land shortly before his marriage he was described as a 'yeoman of Fullwood.' The purchase may have been so Robert could hand on a larger farm to his son. It is not known when this happened but the first reference to John Marshall, presumably Robert's son, is contained in a letter to

Fairbanks, the Surveyors in 1833.

The letter requests assistance in a boundary dispute that John Woodcroft of Manchester, who owned Bennet Grange, was having with one of his neighbours, John Marshall, the tenant of Fullwood Hall.

In the letter, written in a rather arrogant tone to Fairbanks, the Sheffield surveyor, John Marshall was accused by the adjoining landowner of undermining a wall, causing it to collapse, and using the stone from the wall to repair local roads. John Marshall is described as an Overseer for Upper Hallam in 1833 and one of his responsibilities would have been the maintenance of the roads in the local area. It seems John Woodcroft did not think much of John Marshall, for he describes him as "a stupid, ignorant, head strong, hallamhite." Whether 'Hallamhite' was a common term of abuse or just a description of anyone from Upper Hallam is not immediately clear. An 1833 Guide to Sheffield describes Upper Hallam as "An extensive, wild and thinly populated Township".

Joseph Hunter does not record the word 'Hallamhite' (or Hallamite) in his 1829 work, 'The Hallamshire Glossary', but, as that work describes words used by those living in Upper and Lower Hallam, that may be no great surprise. In his 1819 History and Topography of the History of Sheffield Hunter describes the residents of Fulwood as follows: -

'There are remnants of our ancient tongue remaining amongst the rude and simple inhabitants of the remote parts of the parish (Upper Hallam) which are not found and scarcely understood in the more populous parts.'

It is also interesting that Muriel Hall reports Joseph Twigg from New May farm as telling her that when Henry Dixon was considering taking Stumperlowe Hall in 1854 he was warned against it because it was in such a 'wild spot'. [65] Fullwood Hall is much further distant from Sheffield than Stumperlowe Hall and therefore may well have been seen as even wilder!

A completely different view of John Marshall appears from an 1856 report on the Stannington and Loxley farmers ploughing competition where John Marshall (there called John Marsh of Fullwood Hall) was recorded as giving a short speech telling the ploughmen that by the ploughing matches the men had

'Opportunities of improving themselves at the expense of their masters and by diligence and perseverance no one could tell to what position they might attain. They might rise to become masters, but this could only be attained by care and attention to their present duties. Good servants make good masters and when both sides were satisfied things were apt to go comfortably'.

John Marshall was a younger man when he was described as 'an ignorant hallamhite' in 1833 but, by 1856, he was aged 60 and it is hard to reconcile the establishment figure who gave the speech to the ploughmen with the 'stupid, ignorant' man described by John Woodcroft in his letter. Whatever the truth of the matter, John was certainly well-established in the local community. In 1851 he chaired a vestry meeting for Upper Hallam and, in August 1857, he was selling tickets for grouse

---

65   Muriel Hall 'More of the Mayfield valley' p50

shooting over seventy acres of moorland at Redmires. The advert that appeared in the local press invited those interested to apply to J Marshall at Fullwood Hall.

At that time, it seems that most of the famous names from the Sheffield industries enjoyed shooting on the Fulwood moors. These included the Dixons, the Wilsons, the Firths and the Mappins. Presumably many of these gentlemen will have acquired tickets for the shooting from the selling agent John Marshall, at the Hall. [66]

John lived at Fullwood Hall until his death in 1867. Six of his children were brought up in the Hall. Seated around the table they will have discussed the farm and matters of concern in their own community. John and his son Thomas will have had plenty to say about the meeting that had taken place on 30th April 1858 concerning the local school on School Green Lane.

66   According to Joseph Twigg ibid p50

1858 to 1863

John Marshall had been concerned about the school in Fulwood for some time. Six years previously he had complained to a local parliamentary candidate about the 'lamentable' state of the school and education in the valley generally. He continued to grumble at the lack of changes in the intervening years. At last, however, something was being done. A meeting had been called at the schoolhouse where all the local families were to be present. They came in their hundreds.

The early history of the school was well known, not least because of the plaque on the school wall. Way back in 1783, the then Trustees decided to use their charity funds to purchase land in Stannington for the sum of £240. This was let for £13,17s,0d a year to provide an annual income to pay the schoolmaster a salary and to maintain the school. All the original Trustees, and those appointed to replace them, had died, save one. In 1858 the sole remaining Trustee was Samuel Fox, believed to be a distant descendant of the original donor, John Fox. Not only was the school in disrepair but the rent had remained at £13 17s for 75 years, despite rises in rental values in the area. The old Trustees were also blamed for allowing the Duke of Norfolk to obtain the freehold of the land on which the school stood and the charity thereafter having to pay £1 per annum ground rent. The Charity Commissioners had become involved, and the meeting had been called to appoint ten new Trustees to run the charity.

When the New Trustees proposal was put to the meeting it was seconded by John Marshall. A second proposal was then put forward, namely that one of the ten new Trustees should be John's twenty-nine year old son, Thomas Marshall, and another should be Samuel Fox, Junior, the son of Samuel, the sole Trustee.

This is where things had become a little heated.

The elder Samuel Fox stood up saying that he was not happy and wished to apply to withdraw his son's nomination on the grounds:

"I would wish him to keep better company"

Whether this was an insult aimed just at the Marshall family, all those behind the proposal, or everyone at the meeting, is not clear but his application was refused and the meeting went on to put forward other names. There were sixteen in all and they had to be whittled down to ten, so there had been a ballot. As it turned out Thomas Marshall and Samuel Fox Junior were both elected. They tied for fourth place with forty-nine votes each.

It was at this point that the elder Samuel Fox stood up again to address the meeting. He made it clear to everyone that he saw the whole thing as a personal attack on him. This led to allegation and counter allegation. Samuel Fox stated that the rent had now been increased to £20 a year. Others pointed out that this was due solely to their complaints to the Charity Commissioners. They also understood that the tenant farmer was subletting the same land for £25 an acre, still giving the farmer a healthy profit that could be better used in repairing the school and paying the schoolmaster a salary that would attract better applicants.

Fortunately, no-one accused Samuel Fox of taking a back-hander from the farmer as an explanation for his supine manner on behalf of the trust, although it may well have been in the minds of many of those present. Once tempers had cooled the antagonists shook hands and the matter was settled.

John and Thomas will have returned home that night to Mary, and they will have given her a blow-by-blow account of the evening's proceedings. [67] It was a very satisfactory outcome for the family, who still had school age children and no doubt a glass or two was drunk at Fullwood Hall that night in celebration. This would have been in stark contrast to the family discussions in the following month. These would have had a much more gruesome tone, and no doubt the schoolchildren would have been shielded from some of the gory aspects by their parents, but what children discuss at school will have fascinated them in the same way that fairy and folk tales did. The fact that it all happened so close to their school will only have added to the mystique and, no doubt, made the whole incident even more dramatic than it was. There follows what was reported of the incident.

On Thursday 25th March 1858 an inquest was held at Lydgate Hall on the body of Mrs Ann Marsh, an elderly lady, the wife of Mr John Marsh of Lydgate Hall, who was senior partner in the firm of Messrs Marsh Brothers, cutlery workers of Pond Works, Sheffield. The circumstances under which the accident took place are these:

On 23rd March, Mr and Mrs Marsh went for a drive in a single horse-drawn four-wheeled phaeton. A phaeton was the sort of carriage beloved by the boy-racers of the late eighteenth and early nineteenth centuries so this may have been the equivalent of the modern sports car much beloved by gentlemen of a certain age.

They took a short circuitous route, and on approaching Harrison Lane, opposite Fullwood Hall, the horse improved the pace to a rapid trot. By the time they reached the school house the horse was galloping. A servant of a local farmer, a Mr Fox, [who else could it have been in Fulwood?] was leading a horse and cart which he had to pull in to the side of the road, near to the school, so the horse and carriage could pass safely. Shortly afterwards, on arriving at a sharp, steep turn of the lane opposite School House Farm, the horse was galloping so rapidly that it was impossible to make the turn and the carriage was thrown onto just the left wheels. After running some yards in that position, the front wheel struck the high kerbstone on the left side of the road and the carriage was thrown violently against the adjoining wall. Mr Marsh was immediately pitched out, his hat falling in the field and himself upon the wall which bounded it. The animal struggled desperately forward, the carriage tearing down the loosely built wall against which the horse was thrown by the action of the carriage. The horse fell after struggling against the wall for some fifteen or twenty yards. Mrs Marsh was thrown from the carriage a few yards below her husband but seems to have been dragged a yard or two with the carriage and was near the horse's heels when it came down. The horse jumped up and the fore-wheels of the carriage broke off. The horse then ran as far as Brook House where it stopped. The carriage was smashed into pieces and the horse was so badly injured it had to be put down.

Susannah Broomhead, of School Green Farm was a witness. She said that she

---

67   The events of the evening were fully reported in the Sheffield Morning Telegraph of 2nd May 1858

was taking tea at home at around five o'clock in the afternoon when she heard a rumble like thunder. One of her husband's employees working in a field also saw the accident and they rushed to the scene. On reaching the yard gate she saw the horse just clearing Mrs Marsh. She said the accident occurred on the off side of the road just after the bend. She considered the road to be awkward to drive down, being sharp, narrow, and crooked. The witness saw Mr and Mrs Marsh lying against the kerbstone about eight or ten yards away from each other with their feet in the channel beside the causeway. Mrs Marsh was lying, insensible, in a pool of blood coming from her mouth and head, when they found her. With help she carried Mrs Marsh into the house. The witness returned with a servant and they found Mr Marsh, half crouched over, in a sitting position. They helped him to the house where Mr Marsh asked for Mr E. Smith, homeopathist, and Mr Parker, surgeon, to be sent for. Mr Smith was not in, but Mr Parker, the surgeon, arrived at about a quarter past eight, but, within a quarter of an hour, Mrs Marsh had died without regaining consciousness.

Mr Marsh was taken home at around 7 o'clock in the carriage of Mr Dixon of Stumperlowe Hall who had called to visit Mr Broomhead. Mr Marsh had a conversation with Mr Dixon about the horse being strong-willed and that, earlier in the journey, he had needed to fight to obtain control. He felt that the carriage was too close to the horse with the result that the front of the carriage may have touched the horse's back legs when it was travelling downhill on Harrison Lane so the horse had speeded up to try to avoid contact with the phaeton.

Seventeen years old, Joshua White, a farm servant to John Marshall of Fullwood Hall, was in a field about three hundred yards from the road and saw the horse and phaeton coming down the road at a fast trot.

William Ogden, aged twenty, a farm servant to Mr Broomhead, of School Green Farm observed the accident near his master's house. He assisted Mrs Broomhead in taking Mr Marsh into the house and he fetched the surgeon.

Mr Samuel Parker, a surgeon from Norfolk Street, said he went to see Mrs Marsh whom he found lying in a dying state on a sofa in the house of Mr Broomhead at School Green Farm. She was quite insensible and died without having gained consciousness. She was much disfigured, there being many wounds on the face and neck. Her gold plate dentures had also been dislodged into her throat and he was only able to remove them with difficulty. No doubt it was this part of the story that most excited the children in their discussions about the accident so near to their school.

At the end of his evidence, the doctor concluded that the death of Mrs Marsh had been caused by concussion of the brain and loss of blood consequent upon the injuries received in the accident.

The doctor also attended Mr Marsh and found that he had fractured one of his lower ribs and was also bruised about the back and breast. He applied the proper bandages to the ribs and left him in the care of his regular attendant, Mr Smith, who came up afterwards.

The coroner said that the case was perfectly clear, but if the jury wished, he would ask any questions they might suggest to Mr Marsh who, he was sorry to say, was still very ill. The jury (which included John Marshall of Fullwood Hall) thought it quite unnecessary to do so, and returned a result of "Accidental Death"

No doubt both William Ogden, the Fullwood Hall employee and John Marshall, will both have been approached by the Marshall children to see what further information they could glean from them about the accident. The cause and the consequences of the accident will undoubtedly have been the subject of many conversations at Fullwood Hall. The whole story was reported in detail by the local Sheffield Newspapers. Mr Marsh did not survive long after the accident as he died in the following month.

There is a tale of a ghost being seen chasing after a ghostly coach on Harrison Lane opposite Fullwood Hall. [68] Perhaps it was the ghost of Mrs Marsh wanting to give her husband a piece of her mind about his dangerous driving.

In 1863, those that conversed around the Fullwood Hall family table would have something other than Mrs Marsh's ghost to discuss. It may. have been with a mixture of concern, amusement, and plain disbelief when they heard that their home had been associated with what can only be described as an enormous confidence trick. This story was reported in The Sheffield Daily Telegraph of 8th August 1863 and involves an invention known as 'the Great Atmospheric Engine'.

A court case was brought by the inventor, a Mr Josiah Shepherd of Nottingham against Thomas Frederick Cashin KCB, a civil engineer stated to be of Fullwood Hall, Fulwood Park, Sheffield in the county of York. The details of the case are long and tedious, but they centre around plans for an invention to remove the need for coal, steam, or other power to move engines. This was to be achieved by dropping five one hundredweight balls in sequence to create compressed air to power the engine. It is reported that Mr Cashin offered to give £50,000 cash or a mortgage of Fullwood Hall and its grounds, cottages waters and lakes, as purchase money for the invention on certain conditions (which were never met).

Of course, Fulwood Park did not exist, nor do any lakes. Mr Cashin however is traceable to the area. In the 1861 census he is shown as living with his Sheffield-born wife and 4 young children in Glossop Road in Sheffield, where he is described as a civil engineer and architect. He was born around 1824 in Ireland. It is likely that he adopted the name of Fullwood Hall as his residence in much the same way as he appears to have added the letters KCB to his name to give the impression that he was a Knight Commander of the Bath. Someone with that pedigree would certainly need an impressive-sounding address and it seems as though he must have known of Fullwood Hall and appropriated the name, adding a park and lakes to give himself bogus financial credibility in his negotiations.

Mary Marshall had died in 1851 but her husband, John was still alive and living with his son Robert who was helping about the farm and being groomed to succeed his father.

Would this information have worried or amused the real occupants of Fullwood Hall? Whatever their response, it is certain that they would have been amazed by the

68   *Ghost Hunter's Guide to Sheffield Valerie Salim p83*

bare-faced cheek of the fraudster.

The article does not call into question any of the obvious inaccuracies in the Hall description, but no doubt the Sheffield Daily Telegraph court reporter had no actual knowledge of the Hall so may be excused. How the inventor's letters may have been received by Mr Cashin, at the Hall does need some explanation, however.

The answer may lie a series of booklets by David Robins[69] where he describes the first Fullwood Hall postman. One booklet contains a photograph [70] where the postman is shown with a long grey beard and side whiskers. His name was John Westram and he was born in 1827 and died in 1904. He will have delivered letters to the Hall as the 1871 census describes him as a letter-carrier.

John Westram's 'round' took him the distance of eleven miles, and as he had two delivery rounds every day, he will have travelled at least twenty-two miles before he eventually arrived back home. Each journey took him along Manchester Road, Fulwood Road, Ranmoor, Hanging Water, Nether Green, Stumperlowe, Whiteley Wood Forge, Quiet Lane, Mayfield, Fullwood Hall, Bennett Grange, Crimicar Lane, Hallam Grange and Carsick.

The same source reports that John Westram was the first to make letter deliveries to Fulwood. Before that they were left for collection at the 'Hammer and Pincers' Public House in Fulwood, the establishment run by Farewell Harrison.

The Marshalls at Fullwood Hall must have been relieved once letters started to be delivered to them at the Hall. It is a fair trek to the Hammer and Pincers, but it would have been very easy for Mr Cashin, in 1863, to just pop in for a pint of ale and collect any letters with his name on, maybe even having come to an agreement with the Hall occupiers to collect and deliver their own letters for them so they did not see anything addressed to Mr Cashin?

69   Folio 5 'A Century of Sheffield 1835-1935'
70   Ibid p18

ROBERT AND ANN MARSHALL

1867 to 1886

Robert Marshall has inherited the Farm in 1867 following the death of his seventy-one year old father in that year. Robert's eldest son has been given the name John Fulwood Marshall, to commemorate both the child's grandfather and his place of birth.

There is little information about Robert or the role he played in the local community. The local press only mentions him in connection with a bout of sheep-worrying by a dog that appears to have caused problems to both Robert and other local farmers in 1870. What is known though is that Robert was married to Ann and the 1871 census shows them living at the Hall with three young children, Mary, Elizabeth, and John. A daughter Clara, was born in 1875 and another child was born to them in 1878. That child, Thomas, survived the death of his father Robert in 1878, but only lived until 1879. The family tombstone is right outside the Fulwood Church door that faces Fulwood Road. It commemorates Mary, John, Robert, young Thomas, and another of Robert's young sons also called Robert, who died in 1876. John Fullwood Marshall, who survived to adulthood, is also buried in Fulwood churchyard.

Times must have been hard for Ann Marshall in the late 1870's. Her husband had died aged only forty-eight, and she had both a farm and a young family to cope with, so it comes as little surprise that she married Thomas Brownhill on 22nd May 1879. In the 1881 census she was living with him and her four children at Fullwood Hall. Both Ann and her new husband, Thomas, were aged forty-one and it looks as though Thomas was already a farmer as he is recorded as farming 115 acres, considerably larger than the Fullwood Hall farm. On the marriage certificate he is described as the son of a deceased farmer from Chapeltown.

During the Brownhill and Marshall era the Hall itself will have looked very much like another excellent painting that currently hangs in the Hall (even though the area in front would have been a farmyard rather than a lawn). The painting is by the Sheffield artist Kenneth Steel.

Fullwood Hall by the artist Kenneth Steel

For reasons best known to the Sheffield Corporation Planning Committee, what seems to be a working sketch for this painting appears in the housing section of their booklet 'Sheffield Re-Planned 1945'. Apart from the small drawing and the words 'Fullwood Hall 1620', no mention of the Hall is made in the text!

In 1880 Thomas Brownhill advertised that he had eight acres of Fullwood Hall eddish for sale. Eddish is an old farming word for second-growth hay. A few years later he sold his interest in three fields at auction for £300. Soon after, an advert appeared in the Sheffield Daily Telegraph indicating that Mr Thomas Brownhill was giving up his farm and selling, by auction, on Monday 15th April 1886 his entire stock of cows, horses, pigs, and chicken as well as the hay and all household goods and farm utensils. The auction was to begin at 12 o'clock sharp.

The purchaser may well be revealed through an act of vandalism that occurred at the farm. In April 1890, according to the Sheffield Daily Telegraph, the Sheffield Fire Brigade was called to Fullwood Hall, which, it is reported, was then tenanted by a Mr J Hutchinson. In less than half an hour Sergeant Crawford, with a manual and four-man wagon, attended where it was found that a stack containing about thirty tons of hay had been fired. The stack was close to the Hall so it must have been a worrying time for the family. Within ninety minutes, however, the flames were extinguished and about twenty tons of hay were saved. The article states that there is little doubt but that the stack had been deliberately fired. The property destroyed was fully insured.

By 1886 therefore it seems that the Marshall/Brownhill family were no longer involved with Fullwood Hall. The 1891 census gives more details as to the new occupants but the tenant from the previous year, J Hutchinson, was not living there. The reason may be supplied in the next chapter.

CHAPTER 15

THE HUTCHINSONS AND THE HAWKES

1886 to 1897

The 1891 census shows Fullwood Hall as being occupied by Fred William Hawke and his wife Fanny, together with their young children, Florence, Jilly, Frank, and John aged twelve, ten, seven and three respectively. Seventy-six years old Mary Hutchinson was also living with them.

Muriel Hall mentions Fred Hawke in the excellent sequel to her 'Mayfield Valley' book, 'More of Mayfield Valley and Old Fulwood,' published in 1974. At the end of the book there appears a poem describing several Fullwood farmers of the 1890's. Verse 4 begins;

"And Fred Hawke at Fulwood Hall

And Jack Fox at Hole in the Wall"

It appears 'Fulwood Farmers and their Neighbours' was regularly sung in the 'Three Merry Lads' and 'the Sportsman' Alehouses up to around 1970[71] The verses, quoted by Muriel Hall, seem to be an abridged version of this song which mentions several Broomheads, Marsdens and Foxes, all of whom had lived and farmed in the Mayfield Valley since the 1700's. Many still do and their ancestors appear in a photograph of the Fulwood cricket team thought to have been taken sometime between 1885 and 1890. Fred Hawke appears standing, looking rather intimidating, wearing a cap and wicket-keeping gloves in the middle of the front row. Frederick Oates who was to purchase Fullwood Hall in 1897 appears standing third from the left in the back row. [72]

71   Ian Russell 'Traditional Singing in West Sheffield' Vol 1 of a thesis submitted for a D Phil to Leeds University English Dept in 1977
72   Muriel Hall (1974) More about Mayfield Valley and Old Fulwood

Fulwood cricket team c1895

Why Fred Hawke was at the Hall but the enigmatic J Hutchinson was not, can be explained by looking more closely at the Hutchinson family.

Mary Hutchinson who was living at Fullwood Hall in 1891 was the mother of Fred Hawke's wife. Mary's eldest son, John Hutchinson, inherited his family's farm, Green House Farm, in Fulwood, and he was farming and living there with his wife and children in 1891. It appears that it was he who had called the fire brigade to the Hall in 1890. His family, the Hutchinson's were the family that caused the tiny 'God is Love' chapel to be built in a field opposite the family farm in 1853. [73]

John Hutchinson is also credited as being of Fullwood Hall when winning prizes in local Agricultural shows between 1894 and 1897. In 1891 though he was letting his mother and younger sister Fanny live there with Fanny's husband, Fred Hawke who would have been carrying out the day-to day farm work at the farm helped by their young family and the Hutchinsons.

In an advertisement for the sale of the Hall in 1897 it was stated that John Hutchinson was giving up the farm.

The purchaser was to be Frederick Oates who was to become one of Fulwood's greatest entrepreneurs as will be seen in the next chapter.

---

[73]   *For the story of the 'God is Love' chapel see Muriel Hall 'More of the Mayfield Valley' p42*

CHAPTER 16

FREDERICK OATES AND FAMILY

1897 to 1926

Early Years. A low Ebb

Frederick Oates, who appears in the Fulwood cricket team photograph must have had a difficult childhood. His mother Olive Oates was only nineteen and unmarried when he was born on 5th May 1854. She was the daughter of Matthew Oates, a cutler and farmer of thirty-three acres of land in Rivelin, near Fulwood. Frederick's mother married George Thompson two years later when she was twenty-one. Both her husband and her father were blade forgers. George's father held the liquor licence for the Sovereign Inn at Rockingham Street in Sheffield. Whether George was Frederick's father, or he was just making a match which increased his prospects, it is impossible to tell.

What happened next to the family is something of a mystery. What is certain, though, is that within five years, in 1861, Frederick was living with his mother and her parents. They appear in the 1861 census as Olive Thompson aged twenty-seven and Fred Thompson aged six, living with Matthew and Lydia Oates at Knowle Top, Stannington. Husband George had disappeared completely. Whatever had happened, he had certainly died before 1866 as Frederick's mother married again. Her second husband was James Broomhead, a local farmer, and Olive and Frederick, then aged twelve moved in to live with him at Bower Hill Farm in Fulwood. This property will figure prominently in Frederick's later life.

Olive and her new husband were to have no children of their own, so James grew to rely more and more heavily on his stepson as he grew older. Frederick was drawn further into the Broomhead family when, in March 1875, he married Goody Broomhead who was the daughter of James' brother Henry. They moved with their growing family just down the road to May Farm, (probably Old May Farm) leaving Frederick's mother and his stepfather still living, just up the hill, at Bower Hill.

By 1881 Frederick and Goody had a daughter, Ann Broomhead living with them. She had been born in the year before their marriage. They are also recorded in the census for that year as having a son John, and another son whom they had not got round to naming on the day of the census, so he is just described as "Unnamed". His age being given as six days. Eventually they did give him a name, calling him Joseph. His father, Frederick, was recorded as farming fifty acres of land and employing two labourers and a young female servant with domestic duties, so it looks as if he was prospering.

Their eldest son James Henry was not living at home with them on the night of the census. It is unlikely that they had forgotten about him! A daughter Olive, named after Frederick's mother, sadly died at the age of two years and nine months in 1878. On the family tombstone in Fulwood Churchyard Olive has pride of place at the top where she is described as their "Treasured daughter" Two more children are also commemorated there, a daughter Verden who lived for two months and died in 1891 and a son Ernest who survived for five months and died in 1900. The last named died when the family were living in Fullwood Hall.

Growing Success and High-Water Mark

In common with many farmers in the Mayfield Valley in those days, Frederick and Goody took the rearing of stock seriously. By the time of the 1891 census, they had another six children living with them bringing the count to nine still at home, including James Henry. By then, the family had moved on to be farming at Bole Hill Farm. This was a very substantial enterprise as evidenced by an inventory of 1902 when Frederick put the farm up for auction. as it included over sixty-five acres of farmland. The reason for the sale may have been because of a case brought against Frederick by his father-in-law in 1902. The case received extensive publicity locally and went against Frederick, but was, at worst, only a temporary setback.

The progression ever nearer to Fullwood Hall was completed by 1901 when the child-count at home was still nine. The eldest daughter, Anne, had moved out, and another daughter, Ida completed their family. It must have been a proud day in 1897 for Frederick when he moved his family into Fullwood Hall. For someone with such an indifferent start in life he had certainly done well and his children were to become as enterprising as he had been.

It appears Frederick may have bought the freehold of the Hall with a sizeable inheritance, he received from his mother following her death, at Bower Hill Farm, in January 1897. That is certainly what was alleged in the court case held at Leeds Assizes in August 1902, between Frederick and his stepfather, James Broomhead.

When the Oates family moved into Fullwood Hall, Frederick was aged forty-six and Goody was aged forty-five. Frederick had the farm businesses at Bole Hill and Fullwood Hall to manage so Goody will have had her hands full looking after her husband and their nine children who were still living with them there. She had help from her sixteen years old daughter, Eliza, and a nineteen years old general servant, Charlotte Lee, but her eight years old daughter, her youngest child, Ida, would have been little help and her son Albert aged only eleven was also still dependent. Her other children are all listed in the 1901 census as having jobs about the farm. Teenagers Arthur aged fifteen and Herbert aged fourteen are described as cattle milk boys. James, the eldest, aged twenty-three, was a milk seller whilst John and Frederick, aged twenty-one and eighteen respectively were butchers, and twenty years old Joseph and Fred Oates were both described as farmers.

During this period, the Hall building was divided into two sections. On one side was the Hall and on the other side was the ancient part that has sometimes been affectionally known by family members as 'The Cottage' and which contains some very old features not included in the features described in the Hall's Grade II Historic Building listing. They may have been missed because, at the time of first inspection the two buildings were still maintained separately as they were when the Oates family lived at the Hall.

A fine painting by George Hamilton Constantine hangs in the Hall. Unusually it shows a side-on view of the Hall, stressing 'the Cottage' part and not just the front facade. The painting clearly illustrates how much of a working farm this would have been in Frederick and Goody Oates' time. The water troughs from which the horse is drinking are still in the same place at the Hall today.

The painting was commissioned by the Oates family and was delivered to them in July 1926 – a significant date in the family history as will later be seen. The painting remained in the family until it was purchased from Gwen Oates by Susan Hostombe as a gift for her husband, Roger, in December 1983

Hall painting by George Hamilton Constantine 1926

When the wall dividing the two parts of the Hall was knocked through in the 1950s it was discovered that at an earlier period in the Hall's history the two buildings were not separated. The old entrance ways, both upstairs and downstairs, had been merely blocked up to enable the two parts of the building to be used independently. This arrangement proved useful for the Oates and later families as it allowed them to offer accommodation to their key workers such as their horse man, Ernest Wilson, who was living there with his family in 1901. Frederick often advertised for workers offering them accommodation. The Sheffield Daily Telegraph of 2nd May 1908 contains one example.

"Farm Man. Live in respectable (20) wanted to go with horses."

An interesting way of putting it by today's standards, but you know what he means.

Whoever answered the advertisement cannot have lived there for long, as, by 1911 it was being occupied by Frederick the fourth son of Frederick and Goody. By then he was married with a family of his own, and was helping his Father on the farm. Most of the other children had moved out of the Hall. Only his brothers, Arthur, and Herbert, also working on the farm, and his little sister, Ida, who was working in the dairy, were still living with their parents. The 'horse man' was also living at the Hall, as were two domestic servants and two milk men. One of the milk men was fifteen years old Joseph Broomhead, no doubt one of Goody's relations.

The Oates family were certainly not slow to spot business opportunities. Whites Directory of Sheffield & Rotherham for 1905 lists two entries for F Oates at Fullwood Hall, one was as a farmer the other as a blacksmith. It appears the latter occupation was expanding for, In the same year, an advertisement appeared in the Sheffield Morning Telegraph of 22nd April 1905 requiring a good four hundredweight anvil for Mr Oates at Fullwood Hall. The forge building remains at Fullwood Hall. The whereabouts of the anvil is unknown!

The same newspaper carried the following advertisement in its edition of 4th May 1907

'Nether Green Tram Terminus Confectionery and Sweets. Best position in Sheffield. Apply F Oates Fullwood Hall'

This advertisement illustrates Frederick's ever-open eye for a business opportunity to expand the family operations based at Fullwood Hall. How he obtained what appears to be an early concession is unknown, but he would have been aware of the popularity of the area near the tram terminus. A boating lake, pleasant walks and good fresh air were all attractions to many living in the industrial areas of Sheffield at the time and, no doubt, they would bring their children. What better than a sweet and cake display to tempt both the new arrivals and those awaiting the tram for their return journey home? It is quite possible that the sweets and cakes were made by Goody in the Fullwood Hall kitchen.

The butchery business was also developing. White's 1911 Directory lists the F. Oates business as operating from 394 and 502 Fulwood Road, 92 Trippett Lane and 136 Whitham Road in Sheffield. In 1905 there had been only three shops, at 394 Fulwood Road, 136 Witham Road and 128 Button Lane. No doubt the day to day running of each of the above ventures was in the hands of one or other of the Oates' children, but the later business name of F. Oates and Sons may well indicate where the real power lay!

All must have seemed to be going well for Frederick and Goody at Fullwood Hall in 1911 and this certainly marked the high-water mark of their life together. Before their story is concluded though, Goody and her family deserve some biographical details.

Goody Oates

Goody was born on 4th October 1855 as Goody Broomhead. Her parents were Henry Broomhead and Eliza Broomhead (Grayson). Her mother died when Goody was only two-years old. She had two older brothers, John and Samuel, but there were plenty of older Broomhead relatives in the Mayfield Valley. One was her Uncle James.

As soon as she reached twenty-one, she married Uncle James' step-son Frederick Oates. Details of their numerous children and where they lived before moving into Fulwood Hall have already been given but one unusual feature is that when the Mayfield chapel was being built in 1896, various local individuals and groups were commemorated by having their names inscribed in several foundation stones. One of these was the eleven-years old Eliza Oates, one of Frederick and Goody's children who received a polished walnut mallet inscribed in silver, melted down from half-crowns, for her pains. Both Goody and Fred her husband were to be actively involved in the chapel. Fred was the treasurer and Goody is reported as being responsible for the annual ham tea. She boiled up the ham in her enormous cauldron, known locally as a 'set pot' in the Hall and put on a white apron and joined the other ladies in serving up the tea. Fred is reputed to have even conducted the singing from time to time. [74]

The land on which the chapel stands originally belonged to the Fullwood Hall estate but when it was built the Oates family were all still living at Bole Hill Farm (as acknowledged on the foundation stone) and so the land, which cost £23 11s 4d, is likely to have been sold by the Greaves family who still owned the freehold in 1896. It seems the Oates children attended the Sunday school at the chapel, and that one son sang in the choir[75]

Apart from her chapel activities, Goody had a large family at home to cater for. She also had to cope with the large number of hungry farm hands that would descend on the farm during harvest-time. It appears the cellar with the stone table was where all the meat was prepared and Goody will have spent much of her time there, possibly assisting her two sons in their butchery business.

Christmas will have seen the local Fulwood Brass Band with their blue uniforms and silver braid, visiting to play carols at Fullwood Hall, and all the other substantial houses in the region, followed by a small army of local children. Perhaps the Oates children were allowed to form part of the procession behind the Band all the way up the hill up to Ringinglow where a performance took place before they returned back down the hill to play at some of the other big houses.

The good times for the family were, like the Edwardian age, not to last.

---

74 *Muriel Hall ' More of Mayfield Valley pp 12-13*
75 *As reported in 'A Tree in the Valley' by Elizabeth Perkins ISBN 0 86116 596 9 pp 161-162*

A Sea of Troubles 1913 to 1926

It is not known why but in March 1913 the following advertisement appeared in the Sheffield Morning Telegraph of 22nd March 1913.

'Alldays car to be sold cheap for quick sale apply Fullwood Hall'

The Alldays car is quite like the sort of adored car that Mr Toad drove, in 'Wind of the Willows' by Kenneth Graham. Why Frederick wanted to sell it cheap is unknown but may indicate that something was beginning to go wrong in his life.

In early November of the same year there was an unfortunate accident involving one of Frederick's valuable horses. The mare was the leader of three horses pulling one of Frederick's carts, crossing the road into the Victoria Vinegar Brewing Company Limited's yard, in Saville Street, Sheffield, when it was struck by a tramcar. The animal had broken a leg and sustained other injuries severe enough for it to be put down.

At the time, Frederick's wife Goody was already ill and eventually died, aged only fifty-nine, at the Hall on 25th Feb 1914. Very shortly afterwards in July 1914, Frederick had to endure giving evidence in a curious case, given much publicity in the local press, largely because of the novelty of telephone fraud in those days. It was particularly cruel on Frederick as the case involved an ex-employee who had impersonated Goody over the telephone to obtain credit for a very expensive shopping expedition.

The brief facts of the case are that Mary Anne Kitchen (also described as Mary Jane) had been employed as a domestic assistant at Fullwood Hall where she had worked for Goody Oates. She was well acquainted with her employer's habits, connections, and manner of speech. There seems to have been a telephone at Fullwood Hall when she worked there because she succeeded in impersonating Goody, using another telephone, when she called T & J Roberts Limited of Sheffield Moor. She said, putting on Goody's voice, that a Miss Marsden was staying at Fullwood Hall, visiting the Oates family and clothes were to be chosen from their establishment by Miss Marsden as Goody wished to give the young lady, who was soon to be married, a present of the clothes.

Goody was a long-standing and regular client of the firm so obtaining credit was no problem. Mary Ann visited the establishment, pretending to be 'Miss Marsden' and chose £35 worth of clothes which she arranged to be collected later. Very shortly after she had picked up the clothes, the fraud was discovered. Most of the clothes were found at a house in Newhall Road Attercliffe and Mary Ann Kitchen was found and arrested at an address in Meadow Road, Kimberworth. She appeared before Sheffield Magistrates where Frederick Oates had to give evidence. His wife had died a few months previously so it was he who had to confirm that his wife employed the accused up to 1911 and that no-one from the house had telephoned T & J Roberts and that no Miss Marsden was staying at the house.

At the same hearing Miss Kitchen is reported as saying

"I do not know what made me do it. I only came out from Leeds (prison) *on Saturday after serving a six-month sentence. All the village have been against me and the neighbours have been skitting at me. I left my clothing at Huddersfield Police Station. It had all been taken away from me. I was desperate and did not know what to do... I am sorry for what I have done."*

Mary Ann Kitchen was kept in custody and committed to appear at the Quarter Sessions the following week to face a charge of 'obtaining by false pretences. She pleaded guilty.

The Recorder heard the facts and this is what he had to say before passing sentence.

"She appears to suffer from what, in other walks of life, would be called 'Kleptomania'."

The prisoner had several previous convictions and if she were ever to come before the court again, he told her that she would be sent to prison. He then took the lenient course of giving her another chance and just binding her over to keep the peace.

By the time of the hearing Frederick Oates had already decided to leave Fullwood Hall, as very shortly after Goody's death the following succinct advertisement appeared in the Sheffield Morning Telegraph of 7th March 1914

'Fullwood Hall – Fine old residence for sale with or without 50 acres of valuable land apply F Oates Fullwood Hall'

It looks as though a tenant rather than an outright purchaser was found because in the following year on 20th March 1915 in the Sheffield Daily Telegraph it was stated "Frederick Oates is retiring and has let Fullwood Hall on lease." An auction was advertised. The inventory gives a snapshot of the farm at the time of the First World War. The following is a summary.

28 valuable dairy and fat cows viz 16 in milk, most of which are very heavy milkers

2 very superior cows in calf for May, and 10 prime fat cows

3 horses – Very useful black cart mare 10 years old, believed sound. Bay cart mare 7 years, 16 hands, a good worker and Bay milk mare 15 hands, very active, a free goer.

70 very superior white and buff Orpington fowls

6 Stacks and 2 part-stacks of prime meadow hay, growth of 1913 and 1914, about 160 tons. 3 tons chopped oat straw and 10 cwt new thatch

All the farm implements including Milk float cart with 4 ½ inch wheels and two dog-carts, 2 very good hay drays with loose sides and Hay sledge for hillsides

Mowing machine by Harrison Mc Gregor and 2 ploughs on wheels. Seed drills

Set very good plated carriage harness shaft, sling gears, sundry harness

Dairy utensils included a 40 lb barrel-churn, a milk dandy on wheels with a 20 gallon can, a standard milk-tester and milk-fever apparatus.

There was also a sale of some household contents which indicate that most of the furniture was mahogany.

Shortly afterwards Frederick retired to Blackpool, only to suffer a further loss in 1918 when his third eldest son, Joseph, aged only thirty-seven, died at Gringley Carr Farm in Thurlstone in September 1918. Frederick would later lose his eldest son, James Henry, who died suddenly at the age of forty-eight on 30th December 1924 and who was interred at Fulwood Church early in 1925.

Shortly after, and maybe hastened by his son's death, Frederick himself died at 9 Somerset Avenue in Blackpool, not long afterwards on 15th May 1926, in his seventy-third year. He was the last of the family to be laid to rest in Fulwood Churchyard. Their memorial still stands in the churchyard at Fulwood.

Oates family tombstone

Muriel Hall reports that Frederick Oates was remembered by Joseph Twigg of New May farm as an exception to most farmers in the Mayfield Valley in that

"Mr Fred Oates lived at Fullwood Hall in my early days and did a lot of renovations and put it back to looking as it used to look long ago"[76]

Whether those 'renovations included anything in relation to the reputed tunnel between the wine cellar at Fullwood Hall and the garden of Bennet Grange, will be explored in a later chapter.

76   Muriel Hall 'More of the Mayfield Valley pp 50-51

c1915 photo of the Cooper family?

The above photograph is dated c1915 and probably shows members of Frederick's tenants, the Cooper family outside Fullwood Hall.

So ends the story of Frederick Oates. From a very difficult start in life, he had worked his way up to being the owner of the most prestigious home in the valley. Right up until the end of his life he retained the freehold of Fullwood Hall. This was not sold by his Executors until 1931 when it was purchased by his tenant, Arthur Cooper's son, Ben Cooper, probably one of those shown in the photo.

By a strange twist of fate, Roger Hostombe's father, Eric, looked at buying Bower Hill Farm as his family home at one time!

As a postscript to the above, Frederick's old home, Bower Hill Farm is now just a tree covered plot on top of a hill, and all that is left of Racecourse Farm where his father-in-law retired to live, are some of the very high walls that used to surround the short-lived old racecourse that was laid out in the fields adjacent to the farm. Fullwood Hall however, lives on.

Below is a photograph of Fullwood Hall taken from the site of the old Bower Hill Farm. Did Frederick Oates, as a twelve-year old farm boy ever dream that one day he would both live in and, even more unlikely, own the grand house on the opposite hill?

View of Fullwood Hall from Bower Hill

CHAPTER 17

THE COOPER FAMILY

1915 to 1944

Arthur Cooper took up the tenancy of the farm in 1915 when Frederick Oates retired to live in Blackpool. Arthur was aged fifty-five at the time and it looks as though he moved his family in to Fullwood Hall. The 1911 census shows him living at Padley Farm in Grindleford with his wife, Jane who was aged fifty-one, and his children, Jessie, Benjamin, and Joel aged eighteen, sixteen and thirteen respectively. His eighty-one years old father, George, was also living there. In 1911 Arthur was aged fifty-three and described as a timber merchant and farmer. His twenty years old niece Mary Hannah Cooper was also living there and working as a dairymaid.

Arthur's father, George died at Fullwood Hall shortly after the move in 1915. It seems the family came from Upper Padley near Grindleford. George was described as a retired farmer and timber merchant in his death certificate.

Soon after Arthur and his family moved in to the Hall, they faced the problems of trying to run a farm during a war that would progressively take more and more of the young, able-bodied men from the area as part of the war effort. An example of this is shown from nearby Bole Hill Farm where Herbert Oates (Frederick's son) applied for exemption from conscription for his young male horseman. He explained to the Court that he farmed seventy acres of land, had forty-three cows, and supplied one hundred gallons of milk daily to the hospitals in Sheffield. He only had two men to help him. Exemption was granted for just six months to 30th September 1917.

Arthur Cooper would have faced similar difficulties in obtaining manpower at Fullwood Hall. He was certainly to fall foul of wartime regulations. Under the heading 'Farmers to keep lists' The Sheffield Independent reported that Levi Thomson of the Lawns in Rivelin and Arthur Cooper of Fullwood Hall were each charged with failure to ensure that Form DR 17 which showed the name and particulars of all employees aged over sixteen were posted on their premises. Lieutenant Auty, who was prosecuting, said that the authorities were having great difficulty in ensuring compliance with this regulation in the Fulwood area. The defendants both said that they had posted the required notice but that it had been taken down. They were each fined ten shillings. Arthur had just his two sons (Ben and Joel) helping him on the farm.

Three years after Arthur's Father, George, had died at the Hall, Arthur's niece, Mary Hannah, also died there on 12th October 1918. Happier events were the marriages, in Fulwood Church, of all three of Arthur's children within a few years of each other.

First was daughter, Jessie, who married Aaron Thorp on 26th October 1921. This was followed by Benjamin marrying Dorothy Boothby on 12th September 1922 and by Joel marrying another local girl, Amelia Kenney, (Dolly) on 21st April 1924. Joel was stated to be at Bole Hill Farm at the time. Amelia was from Birks Green farm.

In November 1919, Arthur allowed Fullwood Hall to be one of the sites for the first ploughing competition for Fulwood farmers since the war. The last had been as long ago as 1913. He regularly entered agricultural shows, often winning prizes such as the prize he won in 1920 in the 'Suedes and Turnips' section of the competition.

A drawing dated 1924 gives some further indication as to how Fullwood Hall may have looked in that era. [77]

Fullwood Hall drawing by Stainton

Arthur Cooper built up a thriving dairy business at the farm and retired in 1930 to let his son Benjamin take over the business. It seems that they lost one of their main contracts in 1931, possibly as a result of the Great Depression of that period. An advert in the Sheffield Daily Telegraph of 27th March reads

'Milk, 60 Gallons daily, from April 1st or in smaller lots, owing to loss of contract: would be delivered twice daily: low count bacteria – B. Cooper Fullwood Hall Farm. '

This must have been a worrying time for Ben but it seems as though he coped well enough as he was the successful bidder for the Hall freehold in an auction held on May 19th 1931 advertised by Eadon and Lockwood as follows

---

77   *Contained in 'The Making of Sheffield 1865-1914' by J H Stainton p 264*

"The attractive stone-built homestead contains in the

Main Portion - 2 sitting rooms, large kitchen, dairy, 5 bedrooms (one with bath – hot and cold). Good cellaring and in the Cottage portion – 2 sitting rooms, 2 bedrooms, kitchen.

Freehold Dairy Farm

With full Southern aspect, overlooking the charming Porter Glen with Moorlands beyond, at present let to Mr Cooper at a rental of £195 pa and extending to about 46 acres 2 roods 0 perches, and forming the most desirable Estate with prospective building value.

The extensive Farm Buildings include 2 Registered cowhouses for 32, Stabling, loose boxes, cart, shed, garage etc. The requirements of the Local Authority have been complied with. Gas lighting, Mains Water, Electric light close at hand. "

The freehold of Fullwood Hall thus again became the property of the occupier for the first time since Frederick Oates left the Hall in 1913. Ben continued with the dairy round and by 1932 he was offering to deliver both milk and eggs. One of his relatives recalls that he used an old ambulance as a milk float

By 1933 Ben was advertising in the Sheffield Independent that his Grade A milk was safe and clean and cost 3 ½ d a pint. The milking was done mechanically and the bottling was by up-to-date machinery.

In 1939 the occupiers of the Hall were Ben Cooper and his wife Dorothy both being then in their mid-forties. Wilfred Broomhead was a farm horseman and there were two young cowmen living there. The strangest occupier was Stephen H Steel aged twenty-five and described as an Assistant Inspector of Taxes. Farmers are not renowned for their love of taxman, so it seems odd that one should be living there, even as a lodger.

The Coopers were still at Fullwood Hall in August 1941 when Dorothy was seeking some home help. Her requirements were rather particular.

"Refined Woman between 30 and 40 for housework and plain cooking; Modern farmhouse 10 minutes from bus -Mrs Cooper Fullwood Hall Farm Sheffield 10"

The reason Dorothy needed help was because she had gone blind. She and Ben had no children of their own, so it is little surprise that they decided to give up the farm in 1944.

Fullwood Hall was to be purchased by Morgan Fairest and the stock was to be sold. The milk round was provisionally sold to the Co-op. Completion was to be on the March Quarter Day in 1944.

The end of the Cooper era was to be the point in time when Fullwood Hall ceased to be looked upon as predominately a farm, as it had been for around two hundred years and started to be considered as, primarily, a family home.

Painting by J Worthing given to Mr and Mrs Parker

The above painting is something of a mystery. On the reverse are the words

'31ˢᵗ December 1925. From Mr and Mrs Worthing to Mr and Mrs Parker.'

It is clearly the gate to the Hall in the 1920's shown in the drawing by Stainton but neither the Worthings nor the Parkers are known to have any connection to the Hall. A Mr Worthing may well have been the artist as he has signed the back of the painting but who was he? and what was his connection with Fullwood Hall? As well as the painting, there are also several unattributed photographs from the same general period. The first shows a group of smartly-dressed men outside the morning room at the Hall. It is certainly possible that one or more of these were members of the Cooper family.

Well-dressed men outside the morning room

The next photo shows a man who is obviously very proud of his van. It is very likely that this is Ben Cooper but hopefully someone will recognize either him, or the van!

Ben Cooper and his converted ambulance?

The Hall in 1944

The Fairest Era

CHAPTER 18

THE FAIREST FAMILY

1944 to 1983

Morgan Fairest was born in 1899 and was an apprentice engineer when he was called up for military service in 1916. He joined the then embryonic Royal Flying Corps and was posted to France. His son, Barry, reports that, using his engineering knowledge, he managed to reconfigure the machine gun at the front of the plane so that it did not shoot off the propellor!

After this youthful promise in the war, Morgan became a successful engineer and that was his occupation when he bought Fullwood Hall from the Coopers for £8,000 in 1944. He was certainly not a farmer. He was living with his wife, Doris, in a new house that had been built for them in Dore. It is reported by their son, Barry, that his mother, Doris, cried for three weeks after moving in to the Hall for having to give up her fully modernised home.

The original agreement to purchase the Hall from Ben Cooper was that possession would be given on the Quarter Day in March 1944. In the mean-time the farm stock was to be sold and the milk round taken over by the Co-op. Customers were notified accordingly. As it turned out though, the stock was not sold but was taken over by Morgan Fairest and the milk round remained intact, but was taken over as a separate business to that of the farm by Reginald Medley.

Morgan was working seven days a week, designing and manufacturing jigs and fittings for British aircraft fighting in WWII. Shortly after moving into the Hall, he was ordered by the Ministry to start making brackets to hold supply cannisters under the wings of aircraft before they were to be dropped by parachute. To achieve this, he had to train fifty Sheffield housewives in the delicate art of welding. He had little time to devote to farming but did arrange for a new vehicular access to the stables and re-united the 'Cottage' with the Hall as early building projects.

In April 1944 he made a speculative application to the Town Planning authorities to develop sixteen acres of the Oakney fields by the construction of one hundred and sixty villas on them. As the whole of the area had been reserved for farming by resolution of the Council on 25th May 1938, it is hardly surprising that the application was rejected. Undeterred, a further application was made for development of eighteen acres of land. It seems that an informal compromise may have been discussed that would not allow any houses to be built below the ridge line above Harrison Lane or visible from the Mayfield Valley itself. This is reported as having been acceptable to the Council but this was never put to the test as when the second application as submitted was rejected, the decision was appealed.

A Public Enquiry was fixed for 22nd November 1944 at Sheffield Town Hall. It is fair to say that there was a lot of disquiet about the application. The Council for the Preservation of Rural England took the leading role and, it seems as though it became something of a test case in connection with the integrity of the local Green Belt. Joining forces with the CPRE, the following somewhat unlikely bedfellows, all also opposed the building plans:-

Sheffield Society of Artists
National Council of Women
Youth Hostels Association
Sheffield Communist Party
The Ramblers Federation
Business and Professional Women's Club
Sorby Natural History Society
National Council for Civil Liberties (Sheffield Branch)
National Farmers Union (Sheffield Branch)
Sheffield Soroptimist Club
Sheffield Photographic Club
Sheffield Youth Council

As well as the University and local MP's and businesses who put in letters of objection, a petition was also put in signed by many individuals. The wording of the petition was as follows:-

To the Inspector, Ministry of Town and Country Planning, Public Enquiry application to build by the owner of Fulwood Hall Farm, Mayfield, Sheffield.

We, the undersigned, being convinced of the great benefit of Sheffield's rural surroundings to her citizens, and understanding that adequate space for the new housing programme has already been provided whole-heartedly support the Green Belt Scheme approved by the City Council on June 1st 1938 and protest against any proposals to use the area thus preserved for other purposes. We consider that if permission were given to build, in one instance, it would be impossible to refuse other applications and the whole Green Belt would disintegrate.

In particular we strongly object to the scheme to develop any portion of the eighteen acres of Fulwood Hall Farm, the Mayfield region being invaluable for its dairy farms on the city's edge and its rural condition, which forms an irreplaceable means of recreation to thousands who cannot go further afield. [78]

The outcome was that no building was allowed to take place and so Morgan had little option but to make the best of things and so had to add farming to his list of accomplishments.

Barry remembers the extension of the front drive to the Hall being constructed so wheelchair access for his father could be made more convenient in time for Barry's wedding in 1958. His childhood memories include there being thirty milk cows, ten heifers, four pigs, four Shire horses (two of which were named Dolly and Robin) and numerous chickens. The local milk supply had to be maintained by horse and cart. The milk being poured directly from milk churns into the customers' own jugs. The

---

[78]   *The information in this section comes from Sheffield Archives file CPRE/6/2 Correspondence re Green Belt re Fullwood Hall petition*

milk round extended as far as Ranmoor Church.

In a letter written to the present owner in 1996 Barry also provides an excellent description of Fullwood Hall and the farm in the mid-1940s.

When the family moved to the Hall, Barry was a young boy. He would also live there in his later life. He says that the original purchase included the Hall and outbuildings, three Bole Hill Cottages, 45 acres of land, two Dutch barns (one in the Big Oakney field and the other in Park Field, just above the Olivet Chapel). Amongst the collection of machinery was a snow plough. The main farm buildings were fitted with milking machines, sixteen in each building. The machines were driven by a gas engine sited in the little forge. There was also a fully fitted dairy with steam cleaning equipment for churns and bottles as well as filling and capping equipment that filled the bottles with milk and capped them securely with cardboard caps. A walk-in fridge was also part of the dairy.

Barry then goes on to paint a picture of his recollections of his early years at Fullwood Hall. He recalls

"At that time, all the adjacent farm land in the valley was about one third arable and the activity that involved, with shire horses. . . . the changing colours were very apparent when I was a boy. Winter wheat had not been invented. The only crop was Spring-sown oats. Threshing was a communal affair, when a contractor's threshing machine would visit each farm for a day and everybody helped everybody else. Mother was a bit taken a-back when she had to produce lunch for twelve farmers in the kitchen. Our arable land was all the 16 acres across the road. (The Oakneys) It being the flattest and most accessible in bad weather.

The Fairests planted the first field of barley in the valley in Big Oakney, much to the amusement of the locals. 'Too high up' they said, but it was a bumper crop. The first field of turnips for cattle feed was also very successful. We, (The Fairests) also introduced the first tractor, a solid wheeled Fordson. The tack room was the tractor shed.

In the winter time, partridge and grouse came down from the moors to feed in the winter stubble and in the spring and summer there were large flocks of plovers on the land and the fields were full of skylarks.

When I was a boy, a wild cat lived in the area. They are larger than domestic cats. It was often seen in the cow houses standing on its hind legs, under a cow, drinking milk straight from the cow.......

There was a large corrugated iron implement shed which housed a circular saw and backed up to where the top lawn is now. The lawn was the stackyard, the house on one side, cow houses on the other side and a row of small buildings across the front full of pigs, hens etc making up the square.

In summer three polished timbers were laid side by side to make a slide from a hay cart in Harrison Lane down to the hay loft, where loose hay was stored. There was a saying amongst local farmers for the smell that permeated the farms at that time of year.

You can't beat June-got hay.

There were lofts over all the buildings. The only way up was by a cat-ladder. A single piece of wood, about a foot wide with half foot rounds cut into it on alternate sides. The whole

thing was bolted to the wall.

Barry warns that you certainly had to start your climb using the correct foot! He continues:-

Irish labourers would come over every summer to cut the hay and oats by hand, starting at dawn.

The gate from the road leading into a small yard behind the house was used

a) To enable a horse and cart to back in and tip spent brewers hops down the chute into the building below where it was mixed with molasses and used as cattle food and

b) To back a cart in and tip grass into a round concrete storage silo made by Mr Tate of Tate's Gravel who lived down the road. The silo stood at the lower level and the top of it was level with the road. I believe it was the only one in the valley and quite advanced farming for those days, much to the credit of Ben Cooper who had it installed. "

Barry then goes on to describe the house and you begin to see why his mother cried on moving in. Apart from the house being in the middle of a farmyard, the Hall was in two sections, the smaller of which was occupied by a farm manager and his wife, with one of the Moorside Cottage Home boys acting as horse boy and one other farm boy.

He describes the occupiable part of the Hall itself, in 1944, as being quite small with the two main rooms downstairs being the drawing room and the entrance hall. All the walls were lime-washed and moulded cornices were the only signs of any previous style. There was a farm kitchen which had an Elizabethan fireplace and two stone sinks and one of the upstairs bedrooms also contained an Elizabethan fireplace.

English Heritage lists the interior as having seventeenth to eighteenth century fielded panelling. Barry says that his father, Morgan Fairest, installed wood panelling in three downstairs rooms. He reports

"After the war materials were hard to find and it took two years to find enough seasoned oak. It came from Wales. All the panelling was made with hand tools and each panel shaped by adze. "

The panelling is certainly impressive and it is likely that Barry's youthful memories relate to additional panelling that was added by his father. Barry also points out that the central newel pole of the Hall staircase is an old ship's mast.

Another unusual feature a very fine stone kennel, thought interesting enough to be painted by Kenneth Steel. The dog house is still in use.

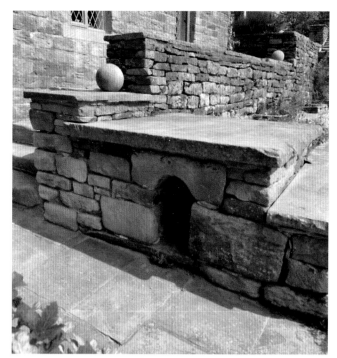

Doghouse at the Hall

Fulwood Hall
The stone dog kennel in the wall opposite the kitchen door

The Doghouse by Kenneth Steel

Barry's description of his youth at the Hall concludes with his recollection of how water reached the farm.

"When I was a boy, spring water ran continually, winter and summer, into the trough by the back door, down to the two troughs on the top lawn, down to a trough in the kitchen garden and then away underground. There was also a trough with running water in the small paddock and one against the wall further down in the field below. That is until the winter of '47 when the road past the house was blocked with snow for eight weeks. The corporation brought up a caterpillar tractor to try and clear the road but that got stuck and was left there until the thaw.

In the process the road immediately behind the house was badly damaged and the frost so severe and prolonged that the spring diverted to a new route and we were never able to find its new course. This had been the only supply of water for hundreds of years and it seems incredible that it could just disappear.

In the summer the farm hands always drank from the trough or took water for their tea. They said it tasted better than tap water. " Barry reports being disappointed that he could not use the water to have with his whisky!"

Many of the troughs are still in situ at the hall. Again, they were painted by Kenneth Steel. Kenneth Steel is the Sheffield artist famous for the British Rail holiday posters that encouraged holidaymakers to experience the delights of the English countryside and coast. It looks as though he must have spent some considerable time at Fullwood Hall sketching the various features.

Two water troughs at the Hall by Kenneth Steel

Morgan, was awarded the OBE for service to exports, but sadly died, aged only sixty-two, two days before he was to receive the award. He died at the Hall in August 1964. His eldest son, Derry, also died in the following October, aged thirty-nine, only a year after his own wife had died. Three family deaths in such a short period of time must have devastated the family, and it is no surprise that Derry's daughter, Susan, then in her late teens, moved in to live with the widowed Doris in the Hall for a few years. Doris remained living there until her death in 1968. The Hall was then unoccupied for four years, although the family chauffeur was kept on to 'keep the place in order.' Barry and his wife Dotty moved in in 1972. They lived there with their children until 1983 when Fullwood Hall was put up for auction.

The Sales Brochure contains a photograph of the Hall, and the sale itself was reported in the local newspapers.

1983 Sales brochure

Through the side gate and inside the Hall, the successful purchasers. Roger and Sue Hostombe, wait to tell their story.

The side gate at the Hall

CHAPTER 19

THE HOSTOMBE FAMILY

1983 to date

Time flies, of course, and it is now 40 years exactly since that auction and our move to this special place. Roger and I (Sue) were happily living at The Hole in the Wall on David Lane in 1983, and were not actively looking for a new home. Having been visitors to the Hall, we knew it to be a larger house, steeped in history, and with a splendid view. When we learned that the property was for sale we considered our growing family and the exciting opportunity of a move whilst remaining in the Mayfield Valley. Roger went to see Barry Fairest hoping to reach agreement on a purchase but was rejected in favour of the sellers testing the price by way of an auction. We decided to attend on the day, but without any great expectations. Needless to say we were both surprised and delighted with the result.

The sale included the twenty-seven acres in front of the house, but not the Oakney fields across Harrison Lane. Barry and Dottie Fairest had moved into the cottages in the Three Nooked Oakney field, and had also retained Long Oakney. We were eventually able to purchase from them both the Middle and Great Oakney fields as well as the wooded area known as 'the Firs,' thus restoring to Fullwood Hall much of that which had belonged to the Lynotts and the Fox family estate so many hundreds of years before.

March 22nd 1983 turned out to be a rather exciting date one way or another- by the end of the day not only had we purchased Fullwood Hall, but we had also agreed to sell The Hole in the Wall to a good friend who had come knocking on our door that very evening.

Before writing about our time here I should like to introduce Roger's family. The Hostombe family. The Hostombe surname is unusual and, as I mentioned in my introduction, Roger's ancestors came from France. In fact we are the only Hostombe family in the United Kingdom.

The earliest records we have begin with Paul and Genevieve Hostombe who lived in the French town of Saint Quentin in the early part of the eighteenth century. Their son, Jean-Louis, became a barber-surgeon in Napoleon's army and married a girl from Alsace. They in turn had a son, Louis, who lived in Würzburg in Germany and who had several children including Christian Louis who moved to London. Christian married Amelia Young and their son, Rudolf, worked for a firm of import and export merchants in Birmingham.

In 1908 Rudolf and his wife Beatrice moved to Sheffield and Rudolf began trading in tool steels and exporting silver and Sheffield plate. After the first world war he began importing ferroalloys. Rudolf was joined in the company by his only son Eric Rudolf (b. 1904) who expanded the business trading in refractory raw materials and mineral sands.

Many years later in 1995 Roger and I were privileged to care for Eric when he chose to spend the final months of his life living here with us at Fullwood Hall.

Eric and his wife Irene had two sons – Paul (1941-1975), and Roger Eric, born 22nd December 1942.

Roger further diversified the family business and he continues to be the chairman of Hostombe Group Limited today.

Roger Hostombe. Portrait by Kenneth McKie 2010

In 2016 Roger sold Minalloy House (the Company HQ) in the centre of Sheffield. With a much-reduced staff he moved his office into a recently restored oak building in the stable block here at Fullwood Hall.

Roger and I met in the summer of 1974 and were married the following year. We have five daughters, Clare Louise, Natalie Rose, Annabel Tanya, Lucinda Fleur, and Sophie Georgia Camille.

My family home was Bole Hill House in Barlow, a lovely old property dating back to 1677 and where my passion for old stone buildings clearly began. My parents Ian (Gordon Highlanders) and Nancy Cobb had 4 children - Alastair (d 1997), myself, Simon (now living at Bole Hill), and Joanna (d 2019)

The Cobb family business was in Sheffield where my grandfather Frank founded the silversmiths 'Frank Cobb and Company'. My mother Nan (nee Farr of Weston Bury in Hertfordshire) remained a frequent visitor to Fullwood Hall until the final weeks of her life in the Spring of 2023, aged almost ninety-nine.

Returning to the summer of 1983 our move from The Hole in the Wall was easily achieved – many belongings were carried over Stubbing field and the kitchen garden, and Brian Broomhead obligingly made several trips around the corner with his tractor and trailer. The eldest of our four daughters was aged six at the time (Sophie was born a few years later) and our family included Jane Pearson, the twin's nanny. There were also various pets and ponies to rehouse.

We received a number of visitors during the time of our move and more than one said that they felt a strange presence in the house. I was reminded of Sue Fairest who woke here to find a ghostly lady standing at the foot of her bed. "Strange" auras but not bad ones. I have not felt this, but neither have I ever felt alone here. The spirits are all friendly – they appeared to be testing us in the early years with a number of curious incidents – nothing alarming though – and things mostly settled down after a few years. It seemed that we had been accepted.

Whilst writing this book I have been given details for the 'Haunting Specialists' who apparently have equipment with which to detect ghostly presences. I thought that our 'fellow inmates' might find this rather insulting and decided against inviting the specialists to Fullwood Hall.

When we first came to Fullwood Hall, the house, outbuildings and gardens were all in need of considerable attention and the 1620 motto below the stained-glass bear in the hallway window here certainly resonated with Roger and I at the time *"And let God help."*

A photo of the stained glass can be seen on page 52. We like the window very much and, for years, assumed it to be the Fox family crest. In time we decided to approach her Majesty's College of Arms for verification and much to our surprise, no records of registration could be found. In order to preserve the crest and in line with the family living in the house, it was suggested to Roger that he incorporate it into his own Coat of Arms.

There follows a copy of the Certificate received from the College together with an extract explaining the symbolism and a depiction of the crest.

Roger Hostombe Coat of Arms Certificate

The Crest

Symbolism

The bear is the principal charge in the shield and is taken from the stained-glass window in the entrance hall of Fullwood Hall, Sheffield.

The five white Yorkshire roses refer to the five daughters of Roger Eric Hostombe as well as his residence in Yorkshire.

The silver swan in the crest is a 'cob' and refers to Roger Eric Hostombe's wife's family, named Cobb, who were silversmiths.

The globe the swan stands on symbolises the international nature of the Hostombe family business.

The sheaf of five arrows held by the swan is a reference to the arms of Sheffield and the steel industry.

The symbolism explained

I mentioned that the property needed attention in 1983 and, whilst taking care not to alter the look and feel of the house, a great deal of renovation has taken place during the last 40 years

Some of our restoration projects have been quite major including complete re-roofing of the house and all the outbuildings which had developed rather picturesque dips since they had last received attention from George Bustard Greaves almost 200 years previously!

Wavy roofs 1983

Some of the beams in the roof near the upstairs Tudor fireplace were found to be badly charred, we shall never know whether the occupants at the time were aware of any damage. Our successors will also find scorch marks on a huge beam in the south gable-end – the unfortunate result of my burning the Christmas holly.

On the subject of fires, it was interesting to learn recently why our downstairs doors around the panelled rooms are so deep and have unmatched sides. Each one is a combination of the ancient original door and one made to match the panelling, secretly incorporating a thick metal strip in between. These must surely be the most aesthetically pleasing fire doors imaginable!

During re-roofing work in 1998, we moved back the big wooden doors into what is now called 'The Painted Barn.' This created a larger, and more useful, covered area in the old arbour. Little did we know what a benefit this would be twenty-two years later during the Covid pandemic – whilst heeding the restrictions we had the opportunity to re-unite friends who had been virtually isolated for many months. They were emotional times.

The Arbour

With a nod to Roger's Coat of Arms, the Arbour is guarded by George the bear. George originates from the Idaho mountains and came to Fullwood Hall in 1988 as a male companion for Roger, living in a household of women – he takes a keen interest in the sporting calendar and family events

When we moved to Fullwood Hall there was a flat roof to the right of the back door which clearly was not original and we restored that part of the property with a pitched roof - enlarging the hallway and incorporating the big stone trough which previously was blocked from view by a wall. This is the trough where Barry Fairest hoped to find water for his whisky – there was still a trickle when we first came here but that too dried up.

Hallway trough

Next to the trough was a round stone window (now with stained glass taken from an upstairs interior wall) which was moved to the north-east end of the building whilst reinstating the pitched-roof in 1999. Our valley neighbours may remember the ancient sycamore tree which used to grow at that end of the property beside the tradesman's entrance on Harrison Lane - its massive girth was held together with a huge chain! We missed the tree when it eventually had to come down and, as close to the old stump as possible, we planted an acorn from "Oakmead"- the Fulwood home of Roger's parents. As can be seen today the little acorn thrived and now we enjoy having a sturdy tree growing by the gate once again.

On the gable end, next to the oak tree, is a variegated ivy which was grown from my 1975 wedding bouquet and it has become a tradition that Fullwood Hall brides also include some of the ivy in their wedding bouquets.

The Round window with ivy

The Hostombe family outside the front door of Fullwood Hall, December 2006
Lucinda, Annabel, Roger, Clare, Sue, Sophie, Natalie.

The Hostombe Family, 1992
Lucinda, Clare, Roger, Natalie, Annabel, Sue and Sophie

In the garden next to Harrison Lane we often fly the Union Jack and the flag of St George. During the early months of the Russian invasion (2022) we flew the Ukrainian flag. This show of support was much appreciated by others in the valley. The weather was quite wild at the time and we were onto our second blue and yellow flag when the time came to celebrate the platinum jubilee of Queen Elizabeth II and we reverted to the Union Jack. A sad period was soon to follow as we mourned the Queen's death, but now in 2023 we celebrate again with the Coronation of King Charles III.

Back in 1953, the Mayfield Community Centre commemorated the coronation of Queen Elizabeth II with a donation of three seats to be sited locally. Morgan Fairest gave permission for one of the seats to be placed in an upper corner of the Stubbing field at the junction of Harrison Lane and David Lane – a secluded spot with a wonderful view. It is a pleasure to see how much the seat is used, even more so since the lockdowns of 2020/2021. It has become a favourite place for a great number of people for a variety of reasons. We have received many touching comments and letters over the years. The seat eventually fell into disrepair in 2019 and, aided by our good friends the Kirkham family, we set about replacing it. The concrete footings of the old seat could not be replicated and something strong and heavy was needed. The solution was found not far away in Granville Wood near Chesterfield, and is a lovely memory for me of my late sister as we were able to arrange for a new seat to be hewn from a tree felled close to Joanna's grave. It arrived just before Christmas 2019 and was assembled on site due to the considerable weight. The area continues to give pleasure to so many and provides a place for rest and reflection.

The seat on Harrison Lane

The gateposts at the front entrance to Fullwood Hall are very old, but despite the remaining hinges and stopper, we have no records as to how the original gates may have looked

In July 2017, I was introduced to 'Mathers of Tibshelf' who forged the present iron gates to my design. Rob and Steve did a wonderful job and their fascinating old smithy was a joy to visit.

Old gateposts at the Hall

At the forge. Roger Hostombe watching Rob and Steve Mather working on the gates

During the summer of 2022, the entire front elevation of the house was under scaffold whilst all the pointing was painstakingly removed and restored using traditional methods with lime mortar – in order to do this it was necessary to take down the virginia creeper which previously formed such a feature of the house. This seemingly drastic step turned out to be a bonus as it revealed all the beautiful stonework, the gentle curvature of the walls, the cavetto mullions, and the fabulous ancient foundation stones – a pleasure to study, and especially helpful during research for this book.

It was not easy to find builders skilled in this form of work but eventually a recommendation led me to David and Lewis Fletcher who did an excellent job of renovation.

Repointing Summer 2022

The Virginia creeper

In the nineteen-eighties we were visited by an elderly neighbour, who told us he remembered a dairy where the study now is and that the old kitchen (which Barry later reduced in size) had an entrance directly opposite the front door. He also said that he remembered all the cooking being done on the kitchen fire.

This same gentleman clearly recalled that as a boy, he had often played in the Bennet Grange end of the tunnel which led from Fullwood Hall to Bennet Grange. He said that it was accessed down steps from below the Bennet Grange kitchen floor, but was eventually considered dangerous and he remembered it being blocked up.

When the most recent owners of Bennet Grange came to the valley, I wrote to them to ensure that they were aware of this story and we were all disappointed when no tunnel entrance was uncovered during their renovations.

The story of a tunnel, or passage, is so persistent though that no history of the Hall would be complete without further investigation. We have therefore decided to give it its own chapter.

Where the tunnel begins? Drawing by Eli Offir 2014

"From Bennett Grange to Fullwood Hall. Bank Field" painting by Caroline Holley

CHAPTER 20

THE TUNNEL

The rumour of a tunnel or passage running between Fullwood Hall and Bennet Grange is persistent. Although, as has already been explained, the story seems to have been handed down from one owner to another yet none have been able to shed any light on the past or present whereabouts of the tunnel. This chapter will explore the evidence that we currently have, both as to any tunnel and as to the rumour itself.

The earliest reference found so far comes from the Sheffield historian Sidney Oldall Addy. In his book 'The Hall of Waltheof' published in 1893 he observes: -

"In this neighbourhood, [Sheffield] as in many other places, there are traditions about underground passages between one big house and another, between a castle and a church, a church, and an abbey, and so on. For example, it is said that there is an underground passage between Fullwood Hall and Bennett Grange. "

The above tends to show that the rumour goes back to well before 1893. This is significant as it rules out the Oates family as the tunnel constructors. Their involvement with Fullwood Hall only began in 1897. As has been described, for the previous hundred years the Marshall family and their successors were all tenants of the Greaves family and it is most unlikely that any of them would have had the resources, or any need, to construct a physical connection between the two separately owned, properties.

George Bustard Greaves certainly had the resources and spent a lot of money on renovations at the end of the eighteenth century, but he did not live at the Hall nor did he have any connection with Bennet Grange so why would he construct a passage or encourage a rumour about one?

The same is true of all the other eighteenth century owners, so we are back to the sixteenth or seventeenth century for the origins of the rumours. The most likely reason for a tunnel would be to enable those with similar religious or political beliefs to those at the Hall to escape the attention of authorities with a different ideology. Such tunnels certainly do exist in Yorkshire, some were used by Royalists in the Civil War of the 1640's, and some by Catholics in the post-Reformation era that began a little over one hundred years earlier.

The situation of the two houses now needs to be considered. Bennet Grange stands on top of a steep slope that leads down to an area where the walls of several fields meet quite a way below Fulwood Hall. This is not a promising configuration for a tunnel leading from house to house, but then maybe we are reading too much into the rumour which may just describe a passage that runs from the lands of one house to the other. This opens up several potential sites as well as the possibility that we are looking at a different reason for the tunnel. Water runs downhill and maybe that is the connection between Bennet Grange and Fullwood Hall? It certainly should not be discounted as a possibility.

Firstly, though we should look at whether there any historic connections between Fullwood Hall and Bennet Grange?

Both houses were likely to have been occupied during and even before the Elizabethan period. There were only two discovered documentary connections between the two houses. The first was in 1622 and it makes no mention of a tunnel in the conveyance of two fields previously belonging to Bennet Grange which were being conveyed to the owner of Fullwood Hall. One of those fields was Broad field which is the field south-east of Bennet Grange. The other was an adjoining field to the south called Daw field

At the time of the Conveyance, the owners of Bennet Grange (then called Birks Green) were Laurence Hall and his son (also Laurence Hall) The senior Laurence Hall was 'keeper of the game' for the Lord of the Manor of Sheffield whereas Ulysses Fox owned the local mills and considerable lands in Fulwood and Bradfield. The Hall family were raising money in the 1620's as evidenced by the number of mortgages they gave over their land and subsequent sales to John Bright of Whirlowe (Whirlow) and the above-mentioned fields to Ulysses Fox[79]. These two were the 'coming men' in the region. Ulysses, at Fullwood Hall, was wealthy and well connected. His life spanned the era between the Spanish Armada setting sail and the execution of King Charles the first. If the tunnel rumour relates to a bolt hole for Catholic or Royalist supporters, then it is likely to have been constructed during the lifetime of Ulysses Fox, possibly when he was carrying out his building works at the Hall.

The second connection relates to an agreement about a well in 1836. The Woodcrafts who then owned Bennet Grange had re-acquired a small amount of land comprised in the 1622 sale to enable them to extend their garden. A bond of £500 was given to the Fullwood Hall owners, then being the Executors of George Bustard Greaves, to ensure that the water that flowed down the hill from the well to Fullwood Hall was not diverted to Bennet Grange. It is clear from the plan on the deed that there was no stream running over the surface of the land. It must therefore have been underground. Perhaps it ran through a culvert and this structure is the rumoured tunnel.

There are, of course, tales of secret passages or tunnels that seem to attach themselves to any significant building of some age. Early Sheffield historians scoffed at the idea of tunnels existing through the solid rock of central Sheffield, and yet in the late nineteenth and twentieth centuries workers excavating the foundations for many development works have come across spacious passages that had been cut through the bare rock. [80] The rumour of a tunnel between Fullwood Hall and Bennet Grange should not therefore be dismissed out of hand. As stated by Sidney Addy

"One is accustomed to laugh at such things, and to treat them as nursery tales. But they merely afford proof of the value of tradition. "

---

79   *See the Jackson collection at Sheffield Archives JC/2/26-32 for details*
80   *For a full description see Chapter 7 entitled Subterranean South Yorkshire in the book 'Strange South Yorkshire' by David Clarke.*

In other words, proving whether anything ever did exist is one thing. The fact that the story endures is something else and the continued existence of the story is, in itself, significant. The story has certainly survived at Fullwood Hall. More intriguingly though it has been passed down amongst some of the older families in the Mayfield Valley. Muriel Hall stated that she had heard the tale many times but quotes one of her correspondents as stating that he used to play in the 'tunnel' when he was a boy. A little detective work has traced him as being a grandson of Frederick Oates of Fullwood Hall. His mother left the Hall to move to another farm in Fulwood when the correspondent was a toddler but, no doubt, he would regularly visit his grandparents as he was growing up. He is quoted as saying

"...having been born in Fulwood and loving it still, I wondered if you knew that there was a secret passage from the wine cellar at Fullwood Hall to Bennet Grange Garden. My grandpa- who lived at Fullwood Hall- built it up and talking to my uncle the other day he said he got into trouble more than once through going into it. But Dr Baker, who lived at Bennet Grange, didn't fill his end up for a number of years after......"[81]

It therefore seems as though there was something there in the early years of the twentieth century. The short statement provides us with a few clues.

He describes a 'passage' but does not use the word 'tunnel.'

It was 'built up' by Frederick Oates in around 1900. This would indicate that the story reported by Addy in 1893 had some substance and that Frederick Oates' building up referred to him blocking the entrance to keep his children out. We are told that they 'got into trouble' more than once for going in there, and maybe their father became fed up of them ignoring his threats and warnings and just took steps to ensure they could not enter the structure! The starting point was stated to be the Fullwood Hall wine cellar and the end point was somewhere in the garden of Bennet Grange.

The Bennet Grange end was blocked up by Dr Baker. Dr Baker was the tenant at Bennet Grange. He was a Language Professor at Sheffield University and not a medical doctor. He is recorded as living at Bennet Grange in 1905 and 1908 when he is quoted as saying that he had lived there for 'many years'. He probably responded to a 'to let' advertisement that appeared in Sheffield newspapers in 1899.

What happened to the stonework of the old blocked-off structure?

In the report of 'An archaeological survey of the Porter Valley' dated 2004, the following entry appears:-

"An underground culvert, which is located in the grounds of Bennet Grange. . . . . appears to be associated with a stone trough/'spring' located in a formalised stone-built setting on the opposite side of Harrison Lane. At its lower end (within the grounds of Bennet Grange), the culvert exits through a 'decorative portal' built from large blocks of re-used stone about 35 years ago, (c 1939) into a short open channel and then a small oval pond. The re-used stone mentioned above includes several identical blocks, each showing a regularly worked concave channel. They appear to have been 'robbed' from another conduit... The pond and the culvert which is of multi-course drystone construction are shown on the 1935 1:2,500 OS map of the area and may be of considerable antiquity."

81   *More of the Mayfield Valley with Old Fulwood* p18

Could this re-used stone, of several courses, once have been part of a structure running downhill in the direction of Fullwood Hall and which provided a direct access to the wine cellar there? It is tempting to think that it is possible. However if it was, we are no closer to finding the route of the same. The current wine cellar at the Hall has no obvious passage entrances but the Hall has extensive buildings and where wine was stored in the early twentieth century is unknown.

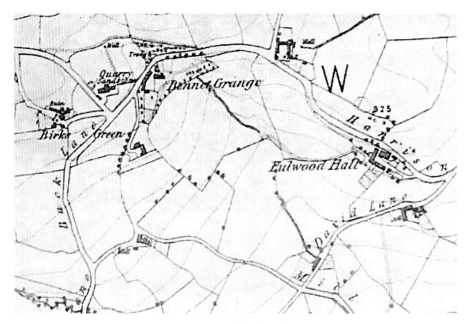

1854 OS Plan detail

None of the plans prepared by the Fairbanks in the eighteenth and nineteenth centuries give any indication of a possible route, let alone where a wine cellar may have been. However, The 1854 1st edition of the Ordnance Survey plan does show some interesting features. The relevant section is reproduced here. The survey was carried out in 1850-1, so we have a record of the features visible at that time. A footpath shown by double dotted lines runs downhill from Fullwood Hall to the lowest point and then a thick double line is shown running in a north westerly direction up to the garden of Bennet Grange.

This is the most logical route for any connection between the two Halls, so it was inspected to see if there was any evidence that it may have been a tunnel or the passageway that caused the Oates children to be told off for entering.

The area between Fullwood Hall itself and the beginning of the footpath shown by the dotted lines has been completely altered in the twentieth century by the creation of a driveway so it came as no surprise that nothing was found there. The footpath was found though and unusually this was not a grass track but comprised a stone path almost completely hidden from view by vegetation that has grown over it for many decades. Why should a path be constructed in the position shown on the plan? It stops abruptly in the area where the thick black lines begin. In this area we found some intriguing stones that must have come from a building or structure and this area may well merit further investigation. Sheffield Archaeological Department are certainly interested in examining this area.

The continuous double lines, shown on the map, indicate two walls between which flow a stream or sough that comes from the Bennet Grange Garden. There is very little left of the walls and the area is now overgrown by trees. When the walls were still standing trees may have formed a canopy above and the area would have seemed very tunnel or passage-like. That would certainly be a neat solution to the source of the rumour as it may have been seen as a tunnel-like connection between the two properties.

Unfortunately, the above does not fit easily with the memories of the two witnesses. Sue Hostombe has spoken to one visitor who said he accessed the passage down steps from the Bennet Grange kitchen and Muriel Hall's witness stated that a passage started from the Fullwood Hall wine cellar. Both witnesses do agree that the Bennet Grange end was blocked up in their lifetime and it seems that something similar may well have happened at Fullwood Hall. In summary therefore we have something that could be, and was, entered at the Fullwood Hall end and there was also something at the Bennet Grange end. No-one admits to travelling the whole distance between the two ends!

So, where does this leave the question 'Is there, or was there ever a tunnel or passage?.. '

In the nineteenth century it was stated categorically that there could not be tunnels under Sheffield as they would had have to have been cut through solid bedrock. The twentieth and twenty first centuries have proved that notwithstanding the difficulties of construction there are numerous tunnels beneath the city, some of which are very old. It is not known why many of them were built. This fact gives some hope that there are still things to be discovered about the Fullwood Hall tunnel. The rumour is as prevalent today as it was over 130 years ago when first reported and the survival of the rumour itself is of great interest. The search for both physical and any other connection between the two houses will continue.

After the above was written an enigmatic discovery has been made in the timber room at the Hall, which is immediately adjacent to the steps that lead down to the Hall cellar. Under the floor of the timber room and, from the small amount visible, it looks remarkably like the top of an arch. Voids in the ground beneath the timber room floor have also been detected by ground penetrating radar. Is this evidence of the passage that the visitor to the Hall went into when he was a boy? More importantly to this section of the book, what bearing does it have on the legend of the tunnel? As can be seen from the photograph, wherever the archway leads, it is hidden well below the current level of the Timber Room floor.

Sheffield Archaeology Department have been asked to advise, but, given the listed status of the building, any further progress is likely to be slow.

Archway below timber room floor

As shown by the above the story never really ends. The tunnel has led us almost to the end of this book. Before we draw to a pause in the recording of the Hall's history though, it is time for the writers to leave the story with a few final thoughts.

CHAPTER 21

FINAL THOUGHTS

Alan Crutch

It has been a pleasure and a challenge contributing to this book. Sue has provided the interesting parts and been the driving force in persuading the various specialists to visit the Hall and in chasing up the reports. My part has been to make something out of the numerous families, stories and information that came out of Sue's initial research and recent reports, and from which I started my own trawl through material at the Local Studies Library, Sheffield and Barnsley Archives, the Borthwick Institute in York, the Rylands library in Manchester, Stocksbridge Museum, the National Archives at Kew, the bar at the Strines Inn, as well as local newspapers to name but some of the sources.

When I began this project I was amazed at how little there was in the public domain about this ancient house. The Rev. Joseph Hunter had a few lines in his 'Hallamshire' book about the house and sketched a brief history of the Fox family in his book about the local Minor Gentry. Muriel Hall, using material from Colin Cooper's research, provided interesting details about selective periods in the Hall's history, and that was about it.

Gradually, the pieces of additional information began to fall into a reasonably coherent form and we were able to construct a record of the Lynotts and Foxes who had land in Fullwood from the 1280's when records began, up to the first mention of their house in Fulwood in the 1390's. From there we have a continuous chain of owners, right up to the present day. Thanks to the Fairbanks' family, plans start to become available from the 1780's and it became possible to begin to trace the land occupied with the Hall quite accurately from that date.

We decided that rather than the Hall's history being reduced to just a list of names and dates, we would try to tell the story set against the backdrop of what was happening in the wider world and to focus on events we discovered about events in the lives of the owners and occupiers. The Hall was part of the community of both Fulwood and Upper Hallam and will have been affected by the political and religious upheavals that affected the whole nation, as well as more local happenings. A little licence has been used in places to imagine how certain characters may have thought or felt about these events, but their actions described are all matters of historical record.

Reading, or re-reading Hunter, Leader, Addy, Gatty, Hey and Muriel Hall, as well as many other authors and consulting the Parish Records of Sheffield and Bradfield, the Court Rolls and Town Trustees' financial records that have been preserved, has given me insight into so much that I did not know about the area in which I live as well as the specific information recorded in these pages.

From my research it seems as though George Fox may have received what we would nowadays call "a bad press" and that the true cause of the Fox family's downfall seems to be as a result of his son William's actions and that Hunter's comment that George Fox 'wasted the Estate' is somewhat exaggerated. It appears that all the earlier commentators have assumed that because the Hall was sold by a George Fox, this must have been the same George as owned the glasshouse, rather than his son, sixteen years after his death!

I have thoroughly enjoyed crawling through the attics at the Hall looking for marks on the timbers and fighting my way through brambles, nettles, and barbed wire in search of the elusive tunnel. Learning how dendro-chronology works and the difference between an open and a closed roof truss are just two examples of the many things I have had to learn to help make sense of the investigations.

Sue's photos of the Hall, its features and artworks and her connection with so many people who have contributed oral and written memories of the Hall have been invaluable in fleshing out the bones of this story.

I am afraid that I must admit that some of the paintings, including those of the Hall's gates and the caricature of George Bustard Greaves are my responsibility.

There is still much to discover about the Hall and its occupants. We are still discovering new information and I am sure that others will discover more and, of course, correct any errors or inconsistencies in this history.

Susan Hostombe

In closing I recall that this book began simply as a record for our family and future inhabitants of Fullwood Hall, and as a thank-you to Roger for our time here and for his continued commitment to restoring and preserving this special place. However, as time has gone by and with the addition of Alan's excellent and prolific research and all the recent studies undertaken the book has expanded considerably and so we have decided to share the story more widely.

The importance of our wonderful British Heritage and of maintaining the lovely old buildings and countryside cannot be overestimated.

With regard to our local area here in the South-West corner of Yorkshire, on the edge of the Peak District, I whole-heartedly endorse the words of Muriel Hall, 50 years ago, when she wrote

"The Mayfield Valley is 3 miles from the centre of Sheffield. It comprises undulating farmland with streams, woodland, and quiet winding lanes. There are old mill dams abounding in waterfowl and on an ordinary day one can wander through this little valley for an hour or more in peace and quiet seeing little of habitation except for farmhouse or cottage and meeting few, if any, people. It is, without doubt, a treasured corner – a magic valley which must be preserved forever in its present natural beauty – preserved without encroachment from any source - maintained in its existing state for all time for the enjoyment of the citizens of Sheffield."

Living in this old house, so full of character, and looking at the valley from the commanding view of Fullwood Hall, her words ring as true today as when Muriel wrote them.

My passion for our home is clear and I am pleased to have, at last, collated the stories and the history of Fullwood Hall ... so far! I trust that the house will continue to be loved and preserved throughout the future generations of owner custodians, and I hope that you have enjoyed reading about the first 600 years as much as Alan and I have enjoyed writing about them.

Susie and Roger Hostombe 22.12.2022

ACKNOWLEDGMENTS

We feel that we must thank our respective spouses for their patience and tolerance with us spending so much time on this project. Our thanks are also due to the following individuals and organisations.

Barry Fairest for his recollections of his life at the Hall.

John Baker and Dorne Coggins of the Time Travellers Group for their views and in particular for John's geological information and Dorne's enthusiasm for investigating witch and timber marks.

David Clarke of Hallam University for his and his partner's thoughts on the supernatural and various marks on the Hall timbers.

The staff at Sheffield Local Studies library.

The staff at the Rylands library in Manchester for providing original deeds and documents and for producing photographs for reproduction.

The staff at the Borthwick Institute for providing so many microfiched wills.

The staff at Sheffield Archives for all the plans and other documents that they have retrieved and allowed us to reproduce in this book.

The volunteers at Stocksbridge Museum for their enthusiasm and willingness to show us the glass exhibits and allow photographs to be taken of their excellent collection.

Fiona Lockwood from Christ Church at Fullwood for supplying details of the whereabouts of the various gravestones mentioned.

Simon Mander for his observations.

Alison Arnold and Robert Howard of the Nottingham Tree-dating laboratory for their dendro-chronological investigation and report on the roof timbers.

Andrés Perez and Colin Merrony, Sheffield Archaeology Department, for the geophysical survey and their time and enthusiasm.

David Cook for braving the wasp attacks in the attics and producing his excellent report and all those others from the Yorkshire Vernacular Buildings Study Group involved in the measuring and interpretation of the Hall features and to Allan Adams for his illustration of how the early Hall may have appeared.

Yvonne Summerfield for the photograph of her Fox family drinking glass.

Jane Bartholemew for her thorough proof reading and general thoughts.

Sophie Hostombe for the final proof reading.

Angela Carter for her logistical support and all those who have spoken or written to us about their memories of the Hall and its occupants.

APPENDICES

Appendix 1 –

The geology of the area

John Baker, a local Geologist and member of a local archaeological group known as 'Time Travellers', has provided the following very helpful geological explanation as to why Fullwood Hall is situated where it is:

"The ground the house and surrounding land stands on was laid down some 319 to 320 million years ago during the Carboniferous period. The house itself stands with its back to an outcrop of sandstone known as the Rough Rock. The buildings themselves are probably made from this stone which will have been hewn on site or locally somewhere from the Mayfield valley. It certainly makes very good roof coverings.

This bedrock to the estate was laid down in what is known as the Pennine Basin, which was a lowland area largely surrounded by hills but also connected to the nearest ocean. The water level within the basin fluctuated in response to repeated fluctuations in global sea level, with repeated marine invasions resulting from successive phases of ice-advance and ice-retreat during glaciation of what was then the extensive Gondwanaland continent in the southern hemisphere.

This setting of swamps, estuaries and deltas laid down sedimentary rocks with alternating layers of mudstones, siltstones, sandstones and eventually coal forming deposits.

The bedrock dips gently to the east and south, so that as you travel west from the house you effectively travel back in time. The fields down to the stream are on rocks of the Rossendale Formation, while those beyond lie on the Redmires Flags Formation. Both formations comprise varying layers of hardness but have proved easier to erode into the form of a valley, than the harder Rough Rock above them. "

Appendix 2

Information for anyone wanting to trace their 'Fox' ancestors in Fulwood.

> William Fox died in the year 1580 and in his Will he named his children as listed below. His wife Margaret died in 1597. Their son Anthony had died by then. All the other children are mentioned in her will she also left a married daughter

| William d 1612 | Edward | John | Eliz. | Jane | Anthony | Lawrence | Robert | George | Hugh |

This William, the son and heir will have moved into Fulwood Hall with his family in or after 1580. His children, shown below will have lived in the Hall with him. His first wife may have been called Elizabeth as, one with that name died in 1606, described as the wife of William Fox. When William died in 1612 his will names Joama as his wife. His children are named below:

| Ulysses b 1575 = Eliz Greene 1612 buried April 1649 | Sarah b 1566 = John Cutt 1593 | Margaret b 1568 = John Creswick 1605 | Judith b c1574 = Nicholas Staniforth 1595 | Rosemary b ? = Stephen Jowett | Gertrude b 1585 = John Ellis 1615/6 b 1645 | Sophronia b1587 = Edmund Wilkinson 1616/7 | Zachariah b 1592 buried 1651 |

Ulysses Fox inherited the Hall on the death of his father in 1612. His children were:

| William b 1613 = Ann Morwood Buried October 1648 | John b 1615/6 of Smallfield = Mary Morton | George b 1618 Buried 1648 | Stephen b 1624 of Fulwood = Eliz Morton 1650 | Anne b 1627 Buried 1631 |

William Fox died just before his own father, Ulysses, so the Hall, where William was living passed to William's heir, George, see below:

| Mary b 1641 | George b 1642/3 = Dorothy Balguy (1) = Mary Pole (2) d 1691 | Jeremy b 1645/6 | Joseph b 1647 d 1669 Lead Merchant | John b 1648 | Elizabeth b 1649 |

Only George Fox who will have lived in the Hall on attaining his majority in c1664. George's 11 children are described in the text of this book and they will probably have been born at the Hall. They were

Henry (1667-9), William (1668-1701), George 1670, Anne 1672, Elizabeth 1674, Henry 1676.

Francis 1680/1, John 1682, James 1684, Michael 1687, Mary 1690.

For anyone trying to trace their Fox descent it must be said that it is an unenviable task. The parish registers of both Sheffield and Bradfield where many of the Fox family events were recorded have a combined total of 265 Fox births, 52 marriages and 197 deaths. Only a relatively small number of these entries relate to the 36 Hall occupants. Hathersage was also used by the Fox family as one of the churches nearest to Fulwood but many important records are missing. As if that was bad enough there are two unrelated families of Fox that lived at Fullwood Hall. The John Fox who bought the Hall in 1707 had no children of his own, so is the only one of his family named Fox to have lived at the Hall, but he did have children to carry on the Fox name until, at least, the twentieth century. Many of their stories appear in a 1982 book called 'A Tree in the Valley' by Elizabeth M Perkins and some others are mentioned in various chapters of this book.

Appendix 3

An earlier illustrated version of the Fox family tree (as then known) kindly supplied to Susan Hostombe by Margaret Hume

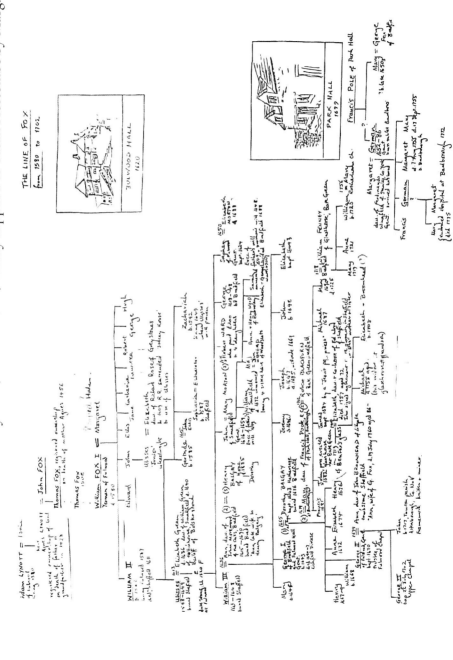

Early illustrated tree

Table of Illustrations